Ron Sheppard has enjoyed a long career in entertainment, and has been tour manager to Sir Norman Wisdom, and a mentor to Shane Ritchie. He has also been successful in health campaigning.

However, Ron is best known as Britain's Most Married Man. He has appeared on *Tonight with Trevor MacDonald* and *This Morning*. The Sun newspaper dubbed him 'Lord of the Wedding Rings'. He has been married eight times.

The Lord of the Wedding Rings

Ron Sheppard

The Lord of the Wedding Rings

Olympia Publishers
London

www.olympiapublishers.com
OLYMPIA PAPERBACK EDITION

A CIP catalogue record for this title is
available from the British Library.

ISBN: 978-1-84897-361-9

(Olympia Publishers is part of Ashwell Publishing Ltd)

First Published in 2014

Olympia Publishers
60 Cannon Street
London
EC4N 6NP

Printed in Great Britain

Acknowledgments

I dedicate this book to my mum and dad, Winifred and Walter Sheppard. They stood by me through all my past marriages and difficult times. I miss you both terribly.

My wife Weng, who has put her trust, faith and belief in me. We support each other in everything we do with so much love for each other. Thank you darling for being you.

My children, for being there after all the sadness, selfishness and embarrassment that I have caused them. I love them all.

My sister Pauline and husband John, who have always taken me in at times of need. Without them I don't know what I would have done at times. Thank you both.

Leigh Ferrani – without such a talented ghost-writer you would not be reading this. A brave and courageous lady who over the past few months has fought through three brain operations and chemotherapy to beat cancer. She has still had the time to encourage me with my condition. A wonderful person and friend. You're a diamond. Thanks Leigh. www.leighferrani.com

Johnny Mans and Family – a good friend and my agent for many years. I am glad you were not my wedding planner. Look how much commission I would have to pay you. Thank you for The Foreword.

Kenn Wu my best friend and you have always been there for me. A shoulder to lean on and a giver of great advice. Kenn knew three of my wives. He knows I am Happy now. Thanks bro.

John Hannam, who always believed in me and has been a great help, not only as a broadcaster but as a real true friend. Thanks for being there, John.

To all my family and friends – far too many to mention – but you know who you are, right? Thank you all for putting up with me and my marriages over the years. I know at times I have embarrassed you and been a right pain. But your love and friendship and has kept me sane. Thank you is not enough, but it will never stop me from saying, and meaning, it.

Foreword

By Johnny Mans

They say that everyone has one true-love in life and Ron Sheppard, widely known as Britain's Most Married Man has eventually found his soulmate in the form of his gorgeous wife Weng.

Some say that to be married eight times means he's either a helpless romantic, or he has a fetish for wedding cake!

Starting out as a Bluecoat entertainer at Pontins Holiday Camps, Ron met and worked with numerous celebrities from the world of showbusiness including talented actor/comedian Shane Richie, who went on to become a regular in the cast of television's Eastenders.

Ron also followed along Shane's path but soon diverted into another avenue of entertainment, becoming a talent-spotter for up-and-coming new artistes, an agent and manager for various stars, and even a road manager for the legendary Sir Norman Wisdom during the comedian's theatre touring engagements.

Television and star-spotting has never left this versatile guy and only a short time ago Ron appeared with his wife Weng on the hit TV programme Britain's Got Talent where they sang as a duo and wowed the audience with their romantic songs.

However, being married eight times is a record in the UK and matches the reputation of another showbiz star, Elizabeth Taylor.

Even American jazz singer Buddy Greco has told Ron that he's his hero, as Buddy can only notch-up five marriages to his credit. A mere beginner by Ron Sheppard's standards!

This is a book that will make you laugh, make you cry, and will definitely make you sit up and take notice of Ron's amazing life.

Having worked with him on numerous occasions over the years, I can honestly say that he's the most interesting guy you could ever wish to meet.

I only wish I'd have been his wedding planner – eight marriages! I would have earned a fortune!

Introduction

I met my first proper girlfriend at 18 and she became wife number one. It was 1966 and I had just landed a job as sports entertainer at Warner's Holiday Camp on the Isle of Wight. Margaret was visiting her sister there and when I spotted her at the disco, dancing to Cliff's *Summer Holiday,* I was in love.

I was naïve and I think I had been 'in love' a fair few times that season as I had noticed that my green coat carried a lot of kudos with the female guests, who, it turned out, couldn't get enough of me. At just 5'6 and with a body like a broom handle I was never as popular as the handsome, beefy types at school. My new-found sexual allure was a welcome surprise to me and I decided to make the most out of it. I was a showman after all and I told myself it would be unprofessional to stint on my green coat responsibilities.

Meeting Margaret changed all that though and soon her mother was talking about weddings. Betty was a lovely lady and being a polite, young, fella I didn't want to disappoint her by not marrying her daughter. Four months later we exchanged vows, her in a white meringue number and me in my nylon three piece suit and dicky bow-tie.

That was how my career as a wedding groom began. I never saw myself as a philanderer or a serial husband. I would have laughed at the notion and was far too interested in carving a career for myself doing my Tommy Steele, Norman Wisdom and Frank Spencer impressions. Back then I just wanted to get on with life and I went with the flow. I was eager to make the women I was with happy, but I wasn't entirely sure how to go about it.

In the 1960's and 70's it was frowned upon to 'live in sin'. My parents were happily married for sixty-one years. I suppose I wanted the same – except I wasn't nearly as good at it as them. My mum was always supportive of me but sometimes I think she despaired of my love life.

"You know your trouble, Ron? You've got big eyes and loose trousers," she said to me once.

It has been pointed out to me by many a witty journalist that I have had more wives than Henry VIII. I have been compared to Elizabeth Taylor for her obsession with weddings and Warren Beatty for his love of wooing women. As I have had wives from England, Scotland, Singapore, Thailand and the Philippines people ask me from which part of the globe I'm getting my next one from.

"Hey, Ron who you married this week? Bridget Bardot?" My dad never used to tire of joking and the woman's name would change each time I saw him.

The press have come up with all sorts of theories as to why I have been down the aisle eight times. Am I actually a multimillionaire and I shower ladies with diamonds? Perhaps it's because I'm a womaniser? Maybe I'm scared of committing myself to one person? Or is it because I love the spectacle of the actual wedding, rather than the marriage? Considering I have never had two brass farthings to rub together and I bought three of my wives' engagement rings from Woolworth's and most of the ceremonies were held at the register office on the Isle of Wight I doubt it was the glamour that attracted me. The most extravagant honeymoon I had was a week in a caravan in Weymouth. If I had realised when I was young that I would also end up with eight mother-in-laws I think I may have thought twice about my over-exuberant wedding endeavours. It may be a cliché, but it's true – when you marry the woman you marry the mother-in-law.

So, why *am* I Britain's most married man? Tabloid journalists and shows like *Trisha* and *This Morning* have asked me the reasons behind my attraction to the ladies and my penchant for weddings. In answer to one interviewer I said this without really thinking too much about it: "Some people are addicted to alcohol and some people are addicted to drugs. I suppose in my life I've been addicted to women."

As I got older this question began to play on my mind more and more though. I do like women and greatly enjoy their company, but I have had lots of different thoughts over the years as to why I got married so much. I was in the entertainment business for a long time and it was easy to meet the opposite sex. But why marry them? Is it possible to be addicted to everything matrimonial?

I knew in the back of my mind that I could never be content and without deep insecurities, not until I had faced the secret I have kept hidden for nearly half a century. It has badly affected my personal relationships with people and I feel it holds the key to some of the choices I have made. Not being able to speak out has been a terrible burden and one that I have carried alone. Being the way I was back in my youth and early adulthood I could never find the courage to tell the truth and it got harder to admit as time went by. It has taken me fifty years to finally pluck up the courage and own up. This is the first time I have written the answers to so many questions out on paper and although it is a relief, it is a frightening prospect, knowing that people will be reading my story.

On a lighter note, being Britain's most married man is a title I am actually quite fond of and I am used to people taking the mickey out of me. It doesn't bother me in the slightest. I would however, like to take this opportunity to announce to those who have followed my glittering career as a bridegroom that I am retiring from the registry office circuit now that I have met my soul mate. May a much younger and braver man take on my mantle of fame. Long may he reign.

Ron Sheppard – January 2013.

1

The woman in the council office building in Bangkok smiled through the glass partition and slipped the papers through a gap at the bottom. Wan signed first, then me. It was two weeks since my mother had died from heart disease and the last thing I felt like doing was travelling from the Isle of Wight to Bangkok to get divorced.

Wan and I had never been well matched so I supposed it was better to get it out of the way. It wasn't as if I was a stranger to the place. When the building wasn't being used to arrange divorces, it was a register office, where couples married in the main function room. Wan and I had had our wedding there eight months before, in late 2003.

"I know you two," said the smiling woman behind the partition.

I thought I recognised her. She was the official who had carried out the ceremony. That really was depressing to me; my seventh marriage was over. Just like that. We thanked the woman and walked outside. Our divorce had taken ten minutes to finalise.

It wasn't that I was particularly sad to be saying goodbye to Wan. She had arranged the wedding behind my back while I was away, booking not one but two expensive reception parties, a photographer; she had bought outfits, rings and had gold embossed invitations printed. I never intended to get engaged or to make her my wife, however at the time I didn't have the courage to say no. She had gone to a lot of trouble and Wan wasn't the shy and retiring type.

I was sad because I was 56 and my track record as a husband was diabolical. And now I was about to head back to the Isle of Wight on my own. Yet another marriage down the toilet. I felt a complete failure.

"We friends now, Ron?" asked Wan in her Pidgin English.

"OK. I better go back to the hotel now," I said.

"OK, you come visit next year." Wan waved and tottered off on strappy sandals. "I ring you!"

I had no idea what I would be doing the following year, but I doubted that I would ever return to Thailand to see Wan again.

Two days later I was back in my housing association flat in Ventnor on the Isle of Wight. I dropped my suitcase on the living room floor and looked at my old sofa, my moth-eaten record collection and the electric fire with a stack of fifty pence pieces on top, which were to feed the meter. It was a grim sight.

I unpacked and sat down with a cup of tea, wondering what my life had come to. My lovely mum was gone and now so was my seventh marriage. I had messed up again. I began to cry.

Other thoughts and images had been circling around in my mind since the plane journey back. They had actually been with me for forty-eight years, but tended to get much worse when I was alone.

My mother and I were very close, so although her health had been deteriorating for a while, I don't think I had faced up to the fact that I would ever lose her. Now that I had been there, holding her hand when she died, and I had arranged her funeral, the shock finally kicked in. I began to feel afraid. That night I eventually drifted off to sleep with the bedside lamp and my clothes still on.

My best friend Kenny, who lived in Singapore, was there for me, at the end of the phone line, over the following weeks. He was a great comfort, but he only knew about my distress over my mother and my latest in a long line of marriage break-ups.

I tried but I just couldn't seem to find the words to tell him the secret I had kept hidden since I was nine years old. By then I realised it had been at the root of many of my problems over the years. Most of the time I was the cheerful and lively Ron, the 'little weedy fella' who journalists liked to send up, or the 'Unlikely ladies man' and the guy who did daft impressions. I was quite used to people ribbing me and I found it funny, never being one to take myself seriously. But now I had nothing to hide behind, no one at my side and no audience to play up to. It was just me, on my own and I couldn't see anything remotely amusing about how my life had turned out.

It was as if there was a lot of pressure building up in my head and the nightmares got worse again. I was finding it harder to cope as the days passed and I didn't know where to turn or how to begin to get myself back on track. I felt as if I was sliding down a deep pit.

I had never been able to open up and talk to my parents, friends or anyone about my innermost fears and now I was completely alone I was so filled with panic I had to remind myself to breathe, slowly and deeply. I couldn't concentrate on anything or hold onto one train of thought for long. My mind was a jumble of unfocused thoughts and images. Nothing made sense. Then the panic began throbbing in my temples and constricted my throat, making it almost impossible to breathe. I held my throat. Tightness gripped at my chest and my heart seemed to be beating ten times its normal speed. I felt dizzy from hyperventilating.

"Calm down, you stupid idiot," I kept reminding myself as I battled with the paranoia that was telling me I was dying. Eventually I managed to make myself calm down by blasting a TV comedy show out on the TV and pacing up and down – anything to take my attention off of myself. I knew I would be okay until the next anxiety attack started. I had had them at different intervals since I was a child.

To make matters worse, the people at the Isle of Wight radio station found out that I had been married seven times and were hassling me to go on-air and talk about it. With a population of around 180,000 everyone knew everyone else's business on the island. My personal life was being dissected in phone-ins.

"Is Ron Sheppard Britain's most married man?" asked the presenter, Alex Dyke. "Or do you know someone who's been down the aisle more than seven times? Hard to believe, huh? Call and tell us what you think!"

Years before I had worked with Alex on several fund raisers and we had become fairly good friends. I couldn't believe that he was laughing at my personal affairs on his show, causing me misery and humiliation. People began pointing at me when I managed to get out of my flat. Soon buying a pint of milk in the local shop became a problem and my insecurities grew.

"I heard about the latest divorce, Ron. Better luck next time," said the bloke who worked in the shop down the road. I didn't even know his name. It was then that I first thought about leaving the island.

I just wanted everyone to go away and leave me alone. I knew that people were judging me and I thought it was unfair that they were making assumptions without knowing me or my past – not that I was ready to tell anyone the full story. I doubted that I ever would be.

The radio station started playing clips about me, which had been previously recorded using Alex Dyke's voice, and they were running them every fifteen minutes or so.

It was a warm day and I was sitting at traffic lights in my car - after seeing my doctor - with the window down when I heard blaring from the vehicle waiting next to mine: "Good morning Isle of Wight! Lovely day! Phone in if you think you know someone who's been married more times than Ron Sheppard! Is he really Britain's most married man? We want to hear from you!"

That was it. I'd had enough. I drove to a phone box, called the station and spoke to Alex.

The next day I did a short interview with him and his co-presenter David Holmes, hoping that once I had spoken about it that people would get bored and forget about me. I was in no state to be interviewed at length. I felt uncomfortable in the confines of the small studio and was desperate to get out.

They asked me where I had met Wan and what happened in the marriage. I explained that I had loved all my wives but the marriages had simply failed – no big scandal. They tried to get more information out of me, but I kept the discussion short and gave them just enough detail to keep them happy – or so I thought. I wanted to be at home, behind closed doors.

The next morning I turned on the radio and a discussion was taking place, about what I may have done wrong to have had so many marriages fail. There were different opinions and theories. I was following a pattern of behaviour. I was in search of 'Miss right'. My mother had mollycoddled me. I was desperate, pathetic, mentally unstable, a philandering Romeo with loose morals. Everyone was an expert on why I had married so many times. I wasn't even entirely sure myself, although I had a fair idea.

I felt hurt and betrayed, so I decided it was time to leave the Isle of Wight. Only I had nowhere to go. My sister lived on the other side of the island and it was the last place I wanted to be. She had her own family and I didn't want to be a burden on her again. I had turned up on her doorstep in the past, usually with a wife in tow and no money in my pockets.

Wan had paid for our wedding outfits, gold rings, flowers and invitations on my credit card and I was up to my eyeballs in debt. A hotel was out of the question.

However I looked at the situation, I couldn't see a way out. Not only were my past mistakes running through my mind over and over, but the radio was still blaring sound-bites about me. I stopped going out completely, dumped my radio in the bin, kept the curtains shut and ignored the phone.

I had let my children down, my parents, my wives, my sister; I had been an appalling person and now the whole of the island knew what a bad man I was.

In my dreams I was being chased by dark figures with knives. As they got closer my legs would buckle underneath me and the men loomed above, mouths gaping wide open, the knives about to plunge into my head and neck. Then I would wake up. But the feeling of impending doom refused to go. I thought I could hear the devil laughing at me. My mind wouldn't give me any peace from the moment I woke until I eventually dropped off to sleep, which was only for an hour or so at a time.

Desperate to stop the nightmares and to get rid of the crippling panic I went to the doctor again, who told me that my grief over my mother's death and my marriage break-up had brought on severe anxiety and depression. I was prescribed Prozac. It made no difference. The noises whirring in my head, the guilt, the feeling of failure and the anxiety were going to kill me, I was sure of it. I lost count of the times I pressed my fingers to the base of my throat to check my heart rate.

One night I decided I'd had enough. I was going to take my own life. So I found my pills on the coffee table and poured them all out of the bottle into my hand. I looked down at them for a while, thinking about my kids and my friends. Eventually I realised that I was so useless that I couldn't even kill myself successfully. I began to cry, bawling loudly, hugging my knees.

After a while I managed to make myself calm down, just enough so that I was able to think a little clearer. My mother was dead now, so it dawned on me that I had less of an excuse for keeping the truth a secret any longer. Nothing I could say would hurt her.

It was obvious to me that I had to do something or very soon I was going to lose what sanity I had left.

I had to face the things I had done and what had happened to me in my childhood if I was going to get better.

2

My family and I lived in a twelfth floor council flat in Kingston upon Thames when I was a kid. My dad, Wally, was only in his late thirties in 1956 but I always picture him wheezing a lot. He had a bad chest from the fumes he breathed in while he was at one of his jobs, spraying paint.

My father was a quiet man who had lived for the Navy until he was discharged because of ill health. He'd been on many great ships during World War II: HMS Belfast, Ark Royal and Hermes, to name a few. Dad was proud of the fact that he served his country and continued to be part of the Navy Associations for a long time. He wouldn't miss the Ark Royal reunion for anything, even when he was feeling unwell.

When I was about seven he became a milkman, but soon had to give that up as well because he injured his back lifting crates. I was disappointed because I loved riding about on his milk float with him, wearing his blue and white United Dairies hat, which was way too big for my head. The kids from the block of flats where we lived used to run after the float, shouting, "Gissa free pint, Ron!"

"Sod off and buy your own!" I'd yell back.

My mum's name was Winnie and she spent most of her time cleaning the houses of the people in the more affluent areas of Surrey, as well as local offices. She was a hard working woman but I don't really remember her complaining about anything, apart from the corns on her feet. The only occasions I can ever recall her getting upset was when I used to pinch the chocolates that Dad liked to buy her, or the times when I got caught for bunking off school.

Once, during a maths lesson, I asked the teacher if I could go to the toilet and then I ran out of the school gates and went home to play with my dog, Scruff. I knew that Mum and Dad would still be out, but what I didn't know was that the whole school were searching for me, thinking someone had abducted me or I had run away. When my parents found out I was sent to my room with a clout and no dinner.

Although Mum worked long hours she always had time for me. We would discuss our day or I'd tell her about the films I had seen at the Saturday morning picture show at the local cinema. I loved movies since the first time my parents took me to see one at the ABC in Kingston. Mum was a musical film fan, too.

She had short brown hair that she wore in curlers and a hairnet.

"You going fishing again, Mum?" I constantly asked her.

"No, not today, love. I've got to clean the cooker."

I expect she got sick of the same old joke but she always smiled. I still picture her bustling about in the kitchen in her frilly apron, listening to Elvis or Bobby Vee on the radio.

My nan also lived with us and ignored me most of the time, as she favoured my older sister, Pauline, and always gave her more sweets, so I thought. She was my mum's mum and although she seemed to put up with my dad most of the time I think she thought he was a bit useless, especially during the times he couldn't work. She sighed when he walked in the room and she rolled her eyes if he cracked a corny joke. She probably assumed that with me being a boy and looking just like him, that I followed in his footsteps.

The lift in our high rise block never worked and Pauline and I screwed our noses up on the stairwells because they smelt of wee. Teenagers loitered about smoking limp roll ups and swearing, while the women hung their washing from the communal balconies to dry.

As I walked towards our block of flats it always reminded me of our school jumble sale.

My mum chose the purple flowery paper and the green striped borders that decorated the walls in our flat. She said it was the fashion but my dad and Nan didn't look convinced when they stood there gawping at it after Mum had finished her handiwork. Clashing with a bright floral carpet, our décor made my eyes go funny.

With only Mum working we were often hungry. After the rent and bills were paid there was usually just a few pence left in her purse, so by the end of the week we were living on stale bread and jam. My sister and I took digestive biscuits to school in our lunchboxes. It was no wonder that I was so short, thin as well as pale and that the other kids would call me 'pipe-cleaner' or 'matchstick legs'. It didn't bother me though because I had my gang of eight best friends and we spent all our time together, playing cowboys and Indians in the local park. Mum went mad when I stole her make-up to use as war paint. I was the daft one of the pack and had a collection of corny jokes.

My repertoire went along the lines of: "I was at a party and I asked a girl for *this dance*. 'Yes', she said 'I don't want it," I sniggered and looked at my friends for a reaction.

"Blimey, Ron, we've heard that one fifty times!" they moaned.

We had no central heating in our flat and the net curtains got soaked in the rain because none of the windows shut properly. During the winter Mum, Dad, Nan, Pauline and I used to huddle on the sofa under a blanket together to keep warm. Our television sometimes didn't work, so to liven things up I sang Tommy Steele songs. 'Rock with the Caveman' was my favourite. I opened my mouth, pointed my face to the ceiling, and began: "Rock with the caveman, roll with the caveman, shake with the caveman, baby, make with the caveman, oh boy!"

"Shut up, Ron!" Pauline elbowed me in the side of the head and clamped her hands over her ears. "I'm sick of that song!"

"Leave him alone, Pauline!" Mum snapped. "He's got a lovely voice."

Although I wasn't tone deaf, I sang like Donald Duck at that age, but Mum was a kind lady.

"He's giving me earache, Mum!" moaned Pauline.

"He's not doing any harm," Mum said. "Be nice to one another, both of you."

Still rubbing my sore head, I smirked at my sister, stood up, took an exaggerated breath and began the chorus again, this time swinging my arms and stamping my foot along to my words. Pauline glared at me as I sang, mouthing: "You wait".

"Kids…" Mum sighed to Dad, who would often try and ignore petty squabbles between my sister and me. We were always bickering. His eyes rolled upwards and then said something about me being a show off.

Pauline was a slim girl but was at least twice the size of me and had a rotten temper. She was partial to hitting me or tripping me up as I walked past. I always waited for the time I could get her into trouble with Dad in particular as he was stricter with us kids. I did my best not to get caught out being naughty and hated to disappoint my parents. If ever I had done something wrong I would always try and deflect the attention away from me and onto my sister. I think Pauline had a similar view about pleasing Mum and Dad, so until she left home at 19 to get married it was open season between us as far as telling tales on each other went. The older we got the more competitive we became.

On May 23rd, 1957, it was my ninth birthday. My mum baked me a cake with jam in it and I was allowed to invite my friends around to play with the second hand train set Dad had bought me. It had one carriage, which trundled slowly around the track, and I thought it was great.

After my friends had gone home my dad came into my bedroom. "How do you fancy the cinema in Leicester Square on Sunday Son?"

"Leicester Square! Yes please, Dad! I'd love that!" I cried, jumping about.

"Calm down, Frank Bush from the grocer shop just rang and offered to take you and another boy. You know Frank - nice fella."

I often saw Frank standing outside his shop, smiling and saying hello to people and I was impressed that he sometimes gave local kids a free sweet or two. He was a fat man and it hadn't escaped my attention that he was one of those people that tried to hide the fact that he was losing his hair by combing long strands over the top of his bald head. But he always looked smart in a shirt and tie and everyone thought he was a kind bloke. He was a well respected councillor for Kingston, so everyone knew his name.

Dad told me the film had John Wayne in it. I loved anything to do with cowboys, so I was very excited as my parents could only afford to take us to the movies a couple of times a year.

Sunday couldn't come quick enough. Frank turned up in his blue Vauxhall with a dark haired boy of about 13 in the passenger seat. I got in the back.

"Hi Ron – this is Dudley. Hope you like westerns," Frank said and smiled.

I said hello to them both and the three of us chattered about which movie actor was the best. Frank liked Cary Grant, Dudley preferred Humphrey Bogart and my favourite was Tommy Steele.

We parked near the cinema in Leicester Square and then Frank bought us popcorn and we watched 'Mclintock'. Afterwards he took us to a nearby café, where we ordered omelette and chips smothered in Ketchup, which I downed so quickly that I got indigestion.

Afterwards Frank dropped me off outside my block of flats. He leaned out of his car window and said, "You want to do the same next weekend, Ron?"

"Yes please!" I thanked him and waved him and Dudley off.

On the second Sunday Frank took Dudley and me for cream cakes and fizzy drinks in a smart café in Richmond. Afterwards we went for a walk in the park. Dudley didn't say all that much to me, but I could see that he and Frank knew one another well and seemed close. I thought the day was great fun although I hoped he would take me to see another movie soon.

Just after our second outing Frank dropped a box full of food around for us and my parents couldn't believe their good fortune. He was a lot better off than many of the people in the local area and often helped others out, giving them spare groceries from his shop. At 56 he lived alone and my mother said that he liked taking boys out because he didn't have a family of his own.

Mum and Nan's faces broke into grateful smiles when Frank handed them the cardboard box filled to the brim with tinned beans and fruit, brown bread, vegetables and other luxuries.

"Frank Bush is the kindest man I know!" announced my dad. I couldn't have agreed more as the five of us tucked into baked beans on toast with cheddar cheese grated on top, followed by ice-cream and Coca Cola.

On the third Sunday that Frank came to pick me up Dudley wasn't in the car, but he didn't say why. I was keen to get to the cinema as my mum had told me Frank was taking me to see a musical. My parents said that it was so thoughtful of Frank to take me out every Sunday. Pauline wondered why she wasn't invited, but I think she was so interested in going to the youth club and kissing boys that was why she didn't mention it again.

I rushed down the stairwell to Frank's Vauxhall, where he was waiting for me.

We watched 'Tom Sawyer' at a local cinema and he drove towards home as we listened to the radio.

"You like Twain, Ron?" he asked.

"Yeah, he's good." I had heard of Mark Twain, but didn't know all that much about his work. I didn't want to appear ignorant though. It was a wonderful film.

"I'm glad about that. I like treating you and your family very much," Frank said. Then he put his hand on the top of my thigh. I looked down at his chubby fingers and at his face, wondering if he realised that he was touching my leg. He was looking straight ahead.

He began rubbing my thigh as his other hand steered the car. I was shocked and wanted him to stop what he was doing, but I was too scared to say anything. Then he told me that he had to go and pick something up from his house. It was a relief that he had to concentrate on parking and couldn't carry on touching me. I remember thinking that Frank was acting weird and that I hoped he would hurry up and find whatever he needed to collect from his place.

I wanted to wait in the car, but Frank said that I would be warmer inside, so he opened the car door for me and ushered me through his shop. I followed him past shelves stacked with tins, jars and magazines, into a back room, furnished with a dining table and four wooden chairs with cushioned seats.

Frank told me to sit down, while he removed his jacket and asked me for my duffel coat, which I gave him. Then he put his hand on my back, beckoning me forward in the chair and looped his leg over the seat, sitting up close behind me. I could feel his breath on the back of my neck and was so shocked by his strange behaviour that I couldn't move. No one had acted like that with me before. I began to feel afraid and wanted my mum. I quickly turned my head and opened my mouth to say something to Frank, but he told me to hush.

Reaching in front of himself and me Frank rubbed his hand up and down my leg again. "I'll give you five pounds if you let me do what I want," he said.

I had no idea what he was talking about but I wanted to yell and run out of his house, so I tried to move. He gripped both of his hands on my legs, keeping me in place, and then unzipped my trousers and began rubbing my genitals under my pants. I could hear his breathing getting heavier.

What is he doing? I thought. To me this man was ancient and I had never been touched by any adult *there*.

I couldn't understand why I felt a strange tingling sensation – something I had never experienced before. I kept asking him to stop, saying I felt funny and that I didn't like what he was doing, but he said that it was normal and kept repeating "Shush". I began to cry.

Frank then held me still and masturbated me until I ejaculated. I wondered what on earth had just happened. At only nine years old it was the first time that I had seen semen and I was worried that something was wrong with me. I was trembling with fear, wondering if Frank was going to take me home or if he was going to touch me like that again. All I wanted to do was pull my pants up but I was too terrified to move.

Frank stood, wiped my penis with a handkerchief he had in his pocket and pulled up my underwear and trousers.

He looked down at me through his thick spectacles. "This is our secret, Ron. I'll take you home, but you must promise not to tell anyone first."

I could feel the tears and snot streaming down my face and I nodded dumbly at him.

"If you tell anyone at all, Ron, the police will come to your house and arrest you. You'll never see your mum and dad again."

Frank was a grown up and I believed every word he was saying. I had always trusted whatever older people said or did. I also knew that the police put people in prison and that they usually stayed in there for a very long time. They weren't allowed to go outside and play with their friends or see their parents.

I tried not to wet myself by clamping my legs together as tightly as possible, hoping that Frank wouldn't notice what I was doing. I said that I wouldn't tell anyone about what had happened and I wiped my face on my sleeve. Frank patted my cheek and handed me a five pound note, which he said was to buy sweets.

"You remember that you owe me. Look what I've done for you and your family," he said.

Then he drove me home in silence.

When I got to the flat I shouted to my parents in the living room that I needed the toilet and I ran to the bathroom, hoping they would carry on watching our newly mended TV. I couldn't tell them what had happened and I was worried that they would call the police if they found out. I didn't want them to think that I was a bad boy and I certainly didn't fancy going to prison, so I locked the bathroom door, stripped off my clothes and washed myself while I cried my eyes out.

Why did Frank do those things, I wondered?

I felt dirty and embarrassed. The older boys at school talked about sex, but although I didn't understand what they were sniggering about I was sure that men and boys didn't usually touch each other in their private place. I had noticed girls but I was too young to feel any physical attraction to them. My gang had two girls in it and they played Cowboys and Indians and got covered in mud with the rest of us. My parents never once spoke to me about sex and in the 50s no one discussed stranger danger or sexual predators. Frank was a friend of the family – a trusted neighbour. I felt very alone.

It was also frightening to me that my body had reacted in such a way, and that what Frank did to me made me tingle like that - even though this dirty old man was making me do disgusting things. I assumed that I must be bad, like he said. I thought that as he was a grownup he must know what kind of boy I was, that he had the wisdom to see through me. I fretted that my parents would see it too.

I was so confused as I stared at my red face in the mirror. Then I went downstairs and watched TV with my family, hoping that they didn't notice that I'd been crying.

Later I announced that I wanted to go to bed to read. My parents said goodnight and I was relieved that they hadn't picked up on anything new and strange about me. I wondered if I seemed different now.

My main worry was the police though, so I quickly got into my pyjamas and curled up under the blanket with my book, desperately trying to block out the memories. I prayed to God that no one found out about what I had just done with Frank. I said how sorry I was for being a bad boy and I hoped that God would forgive me.

It was the night before school on the Monday and I eventually dozed off as it was getting light. The only time I felt safe to sleep properly was at my school desk at the back of the class. Luckily my teacher didn't notice. She was used to me staring gormlessly out of the window or mimicking her Scottish accent to make my classmates laugh so if she did spot me she was probably glad of some peace.

When I got home that day Dad gave me the horrifying news that Frank had called and was taking me out again the following Sunday. I felt sick and tried to think of an excuse not to go.

"Frank has been very good to this family, son. It'll seem ungrateful if you don't go," Dad said. Mum and Nan agreed with him. I was trapped.

That week Frank sent another box of groceries around for us and as Mum dished up corned beef hash, followed by steamed pudding I felt like throwing mine in the bin.

"Yum!" Pauline exclaimed, spooning the sticky dessert into her mouth. I dropped my spoon and stared down at my plate, numb with dread and fear. Sunday afternoon was looming.

I was a nervous wreck at school and my friends wondered why I was so quiet and in no mood to race about, playing Cowboys and Indians. My mum touched my forehead, checking to see if I had a temperature, she was so used to hearing me sing or asking to play outside with my gang. My friend, Loretta, asked me what was wrong, but I just shook my head. The only time I spoke about my fears was when I was in my bedroom with Scruff and my teddy, Marlon. I told them everything.

Frank was there on the dot – 2pm - sitting outside in his blue Vauxhall in his diamond-patterned tie, smiling at me as I sauntered to his car and got in. He tried to make conversation on the way to the cinema, but my tongue was stuck to the roof of my mouth. All I could think about was what had happened the Sunday before and whether he was going to do that horrible stuff to me again.

After the movie Frank told me he was taking me to his house. I knew what was going to happen and he ignored all my protests in the car on the way over.

"I want to go home," I cried, tears running down my face.

"Stop that fussing, Ron. It'll be fine," he snapped.

When we got there Frank pulled my trousers and pants down, sat me on the chair and began rubbing me. I started to cry again and said I didn't want him to touch me in my private place, but he said that if I didn't let him he would tell the police about what a naughty boy I was and that my parents would hate me.

When he had finally made me erect, Frank led me over to the corner of the room, reached for his camera from off a shelf and took pictures of my genitals, while I stood there shaking. When I put my hands in front of myself to try and hide my embarrassment Frank pushed them aside and snapped, "Do as you're told, Ron!"

Then he said that he was going to suck my penis. I was horrified. Why would anyone do that? I didn't want this old man putting my penis in his mouth and I said "no, I won't let you."

Frank pulled my hands away from me, which I was still using to shield my genital area.

"If you don't let me suck you, Ron, I'll show these pictures to the police, the newspapers and your parents," Frank warned.

I had no choice but to do as I was told. The thought of my family and friends at school seeing the photos was shameful. Frank then knelt down and performed oral sex on me, biting me when I tried to pull away. I yelped with pain as tears streamed down my face. I repeatedly begged him to stop, but he wouldn't let me go until I had ejaculated into his mouth. He then wiped me with his handkerchief, pulled my clothes back up and gave me a five pound note.

"Buy yourself some sweets," he said.

For the next six years Sunday afternoons were a nightmare for me.

3

One day Dad came in with a cine-projector he had been saving up for. He was very proud of his new contraption and I was fascinated, watching him as he put it all together and it made a whirring sound, while he talked excitedly of the things we could watch on it. He then stopped and went quiet.

"You alright, Dad?" I asked and put my hand on his arm.

He waggled a finger in my face: "Ron, don't you fiddle about with this. It's not a toy!"

"Course not," I replied.

"I mean it," he warned.

I had unintentionally broken many ornaments and other objects in the house so I knew Dad meant business this time. But, being warned not to play with something, made it all the more tempting for me. The urge to go and do exactly what I had been told not to was too overwhelming – such as the time I fell off a narrow wall into a neighbour's garden, flattening his roses. This was after both parents had nagged me not to bother the neighbours on countless occasions – especially Mr. Mitchell.

Mr. Mitchell lived in one of the nicer houses further down our street and had been watching me out of his living room window and had come flying out of his front door as I crashed onto his prize blooms. Seeing his 25-stone bulk wheezing towards me, I ran home and hid in my bedroom, hoping he would be too fat to make it all the way up the stairs to our 12th floor flat to tell my parents and land me in it. But eventually I heard a knock at the front door, followed by raised voices. I edged out into the hallway a little and heard Dad say, "Sorry, Mr. Mitchell. Ron won't do it again, I promise."

"He better not or I'll knock his bloody block off next time! I'm sick of the kids 'round 'ere!" Mr Mitchell barked.

When Mr. Mitchell stormed off home, Dad shouted at me to do as I was told for once. He seethed: "Cause trouble again and you'll bloody well know about it, boy!"

I watched my dad place his precious cine-projector in its cardboard box in his bedroom wardrobe, on top of a pile of tank tops, and I waited patiently until everyone was out until I crept into his bedroom, double-checking that Nan and Pauline weren't skulking about. I took the projector out of the wardrobe and began playing with it, fiddling with the buttons and trying to understand how it worked. I gave it a good shake and held it up to the light coming in through the window. Scruff trotted into the room and as I chased him around the bed, pretending to be a cowboy, the projector accidentally fell out of my hands and crashed onto the floor. I stood there, open-mouthed. Knowing how furious Dad was going to be I felt my fear rise and I stuffed it back in its box and threw it back in its original place, hoping no one would notice that its arm was hanging off. When Dad came home later that day I sat nervously on the sofa, praying he wouldn't look at his projector. Unfortunately it was one of the first things he did. I sloped off towards my bedroom to hide.

"Ron..." I heard his voice boom down the hallway. "Come in here a minute please..."

"Yes, Dad?" I said and edged into his bedroom. He was dangling the broken projector in front of him. His lips always went white and pinched when he was angry and his blond eyebrows bunched together in a deep frown.

"Did you do this?"

"What?"

"This!" He pointed at the broken arm on the contraption.

"No, Dad."

Sometimes he would use a belt to hit us with, although only when we had been particularly naughty, but I knew this was a situation that would merit a fairly good thrashing if I was found out. I gulped. Dad was a short, skinny bloke but when in a temper he seemed big and intimidating. I decided to carry on pleading ignorance, claiming that it had nothing to do with me. I said that I had been outside playing football with my friends Paul and Geoff and that I would go and get them and he could ask them about it if he didn't believe me. I hoped that he wouldn't call my bluff.

"Why's it broken then?" Dad asked.

I shrugged.

"*Ron…*"

"Well, I didn't really want to have to tell you this, Dad… but…"

"*Ron…*"

"Pauline did it," I said.

That evening, when my sister got in from the youth club, she got the belt and was grounded. I did feel a bit guilty but I reasoned that as she was older than me by six years that she wouldn't mind as much as I would, me being smaller. When Pauline got me alone in the kitchen she grabbed me by the front of my t-shirt and shook me so hard that my teeth clanked together. She held me against the sink unit with one hand and the other was raised into a bunched fist, as if she was about to punch me.

"I know it was you, Ron," she said. "I'll get you back for this!"

I chewed my finger nails. "I'm *really* scared."

Pauline whacked me around the ear and stormed off, promising me that I hadn't heard the last of it.

My sister had gone through phases of taking up hockey and ballet during her childhood, but as she reached 14 she preferred to hang out with her friends, flirting with older boys. At 16 she had a steady boyfriend and spent most evenings with him. Now she was grounded it meant that she wouldn't be able to see him for a week. Every time we bumped into each other in the house she threw me a filthy look or put her foot out to trip me up whenever I walked past.

The next night she slumped down on the sofa, where I was lying, watching TV. I managed to drag my legs out from under her and I could see from her stern profile and crossed arms that she was still angry with me, so I gently tapped her arm and said: "I bet you wish you were kissing that big girl's blouse now, eh?"

"I'm warning you, Ron!" Pauline yelled.

I held my arm out in an effeminate manner and put on a woman's voice; "My name's John and I'm a girl!"

"Just 'cos he has long hair doesn't make him a girl!" she shouted. "*Mum!*"

"He's a big girl! He's a big girl!" I carried on and began jumping up and down on the sofa, singing: "Pauline's boyfriend's a woman!"

My sister screamed that she was sick to death of me, stood, grabbed my arm and with an almighty grunt she flung me across the room. The pain on landing was excruciating and I wailed until Mum and Dad ran into the room. Dad could see that my arm was turning a funny colour and asked one of the neighbours to take us to hospital. When we got there I was given an x-ray. I had broken a bone. When we returned home, Pauline came into my room, where I lay on the bed with my arm in a sling, clutching my teddy, Marlon.

"Get out," I said and turned my back on her. Scruff was sprawled across my blankets and made a groaning sound in his sleep.

"These are for you," she said quietly. I faced her and watched as she held her hand out flat. I saw one and a half sticks of Juicy Fruit chewing gum.

"Why's there only half left of that one?" I asked, nodding at the contents of her hand.

"Do you want it or not?"

"Go on then." I grabbed the gum, unwrapped it and shoved it into my mouth quickly, in case she asked for it back. Pauline left my room and shut the door. I felt very smug. I had some gum and a new plaster cast. That meant Mum would let me have a few days off school.

4

Life at home in 1958 was pretty much the same on the surface; I got great satisfaction out of annoying my sister and spent most of my time larking about with my friends, but inside I knew I was different now. I carried around a strange feeling of detachment from the world.

No one knew my secret and Frank continued to drum it into me every Sunday that no one must find out about it either. I often asked myself why I was different. Why had Frank chosen me? Why was I so bad that he had to do those things to me? I had seen movies in which criminals were thrown in jail cells by the police, so I knew what was in store for me if I did tell. For a 10-year-old my secret was a huge one to carry and as each Sunday loomed I spent more and more time alone or down by the pond in the local park, watching the ducks and the fishermen sitting on the bank, no doubt escaping wives and families. I would laugh at the ducks' constant quacking and fighting over old sandwich crusts people threw at them and if I had any spare bread from my school lunch box I'd share it with them.

The park and duck pond helped take my mind off of what was going on in my life. Frank couldn't find me there. I wasn't safe with my family at home; Frank still sent boxes of food around every week and called my parents, asking for permission to take me out. I lost count of the times that they would tell me how lucky I was, even though every Saturday I pretended to be ill, each weekend coming up with a new affliction. I was told "not to be so silly" as Mum checked that I was wearing my best jumper and that I had washed my neck before the Sunday outings. Then she'd walk downstairs with me and wave and smile, watching Frank drive off with me in his car. All the while I would be screaming "help me, Mum!" in my head until we turned the corner and were out of sight. I hoped she would save me.

My parents simply thought I was being an awkward kid who would rather be out playing football with his mates. To them and everyone else in the area Frank Bush was a pillar of the community and my parents were terrified of offending such a respected man. They also needed the food parcels that now bulged with bacon, chocolate biscuits, coffee and assorted vegetables that they couldn't afford to buy.

I never saw any of the movies that played on the big screen in front of me during those cinema visits with Frank, and often Dudley, who I assumed was going through the same ordeal as me, but we never really talked that much. Frank used to tell the two of us to call him 'Uncle' when we were out and when I first met the pair of them I wondered if they were related. As time went on it became obvious to me that Dudley was just another kid from a poor family that Frank was using.

All I could focus on during those films was Frank's breathing or him chewing popcorn loudly. I would look at his fat hands on the arm rests of the seats imagining what they would be doing to me later. I was so paralysed with fear that even John Wayne or Tommy Steele couldn't jolt me out of my panic. When the movie credits rolled I became so scared that I was desperate to cling on to the neck of someone sitting in front of me and to shout "please help me!" but I didn't dare.

When the three of us left the cinema, Frank dropped Dudley off and then we always went back to his house, only Frank stopped using the excuse that he wanted to pick something up at home. By now it was just expected of me to go with him. When he demanded that I touch him I always refused and cried so much that he was eventually content to make do with performing sex acts on me.

The second and last time he made me pose for photographs was a few months after the first incident. I kept my hands clamped tightly onto the waistband of my trousers, but Frank prized them off and slapped them away. He yanked my trousers and pants down to the floor and pushed me into the wall.

"Stand still, Ron," Frank snapped. "I want some good shots this time."

While he clicked away, the flash made me blink wildly. I could see Frank's fat belly underneath the camera and it was all I could concentrate on. He was wearing a blue shirt and his pale flesh poked out of the straining gaps in between the buttons.

"Good, Ron. Good Boy," he said. "That's nice."

Eventually he stopped taking pictures, and still with my clothes bunched around my ankles, he pulled me onto one of the hardback chairs he always preferred to use, knelt down and performed oral sex on me, ignoring my pleas for him to stop, as always. He wiped my semen from his lips and gave me some money to buy sweets.

It was the same every single Sunday, but it was the last time he took photos of me. Knowing that he had such pictures was enough to keep me in line though. He often threatened to get them published in the local paper.

"Come on, let's get your coat on and I'll take you home," he said, as if what had happened was perfectly normal. I was crying and needed to wipe my nose.

"Stop that blubbing, will you?" he shouted. "Do you want people to find out about us? Do you?"

I was sobbing so hard that I couldn't answer him.

"Do you want all your friends to know that you're a bad boy?"

"No," I said.

"Well stop that crying then. This is the way things are. I do a lot for your family. You owe me and this is how you pay me back. Once a week won't kill you will it?"

But that's what it felt like. I sometimes thought I would have been better off dead.

We were silent in the car on the way back to my home and I can vividly remember staring out of the passenger window, at other people's passing houses. I wondered how these strangers lived and if their lives were like mine. Did they do what Frank and I were doing, too? How I wished I could be someone else; anyone but me.

It was only when I was at the duck pond that I felt free. I used to spend hours looking at the small grassy island in the middle of that big pond, wondering what it would be like to build a shed there and live in it. Once I decided to try swimming to the island but I got entangled with an old pram someone had thrown in the pond. On other days I would dangle a bit of wire into the water with a worm on the end, hoping to catch a fish.

Soon my friends began to notice that I was spending more time on my own during school playtimes and while I did join in with games of Cowboys and Indians I think they could tell that my heart wasn't in it anymore. I still larked about but there were situations when my worries would overshadow everything else and I would retreat into myself. I don't think I was aware that I had changed.

"You all right, Ron?" My best friend Paul asked and sat down next to me. I was sitting cross-legged and absent-mindedly pulling blades of grass out of the ground. It was lunchtime and all the kids were tearing about in the sun with a ball. Paul had a burnt nose which looked funny against his freckles. A blond athletic kid, he was football mad, like me. He prodded a small stick at the dry earth.

"Yeah, course," I replied.

"You seem quiet."

"Do I?" I felt my face flush. Did Paul know something was different about me now? We'd been close since infant school.

"Yeah," he said. "Is there something wrong?"

"Nah."

"Sure?"

"Let's go play with the others!" I stood up and ran towards the rest of the gang who were running about shrieking. Paul gently thumped me on the back and sprinted ahead.

The sexual abuse had been happening every Sunday for almost two years when I left junior school and started at Richmond Road Secondary Modern in Kingston, Surrey, when I was 11. It was a typical-looking school building: red brick, bike sheds at the front, prefab classrooms down one end to provide more space for lessons, unsmiling teachers walking about in pairs, clutching books.

From my first day I hated it there and soon I was bunking off as much as I possibly could. The place was big on sports and I had rugby on a Tuesday and cross country every Thursday. The only game I was ever interested in was football and back when I was nine I won my first medal when my team won the school league. That was a proud day. Sports at senior school was a different matter though.

The first time I was in the changing room with 20 or 30 other kids getting into their rugby kit I froze. I couldn't let anyone see me naked and I felt the tears well up in my eyes. The urge to run out of school and hide was overwhelming, but the teacher had already spotted me.

"Hurry up and get undressed, Ron," ordered Mr. Davies, the sports master. "Time to get out on the field! Chop, chop!"

The other boys looked over at me while I clung to my school bag, my head lowered to hide my tears. A couple of them laughed and whispered. I knew I had to do something or the situation was going to get out of hand. Teachers in those days had no problem with manhandling or smacking kids who refused to do as they were told. The last thing I wanted was any more attention focused on me.

"Yes, sir," I muttered.

I slowly took my duffle coat off and hung it on a hook, put my bag on one of the wooden benches in the changing room and pulled out my rugby kit with shaking hands.

Over the previous few years I had been suffering from anxiety and what I realised as I got older were panic attacks, usually in my bed at night, before I fell asleep. I had hidden my anxiety and nightmares from my parents, although they kept asking me why I cried out in my sleep. I said I didn't know and couldn't recall what I dreamt about. But I remembered. The dreams were nearly always the same. I was being chased, pitch black all around me, and then I was suffocating, falling into darkness, a man following behind muttering "Ron... where you going, Ron?" Then the man would turn to look at me and it was Frank, except he looked different to the non-descript, bespectacled middle aged man I knew. He was bigger and more threatening, almost wolfish. Perhaps I watched too many monster movies. Frank's appearance often changed in my nightmares, but he was always took a malevolent form. Sometimes it would be a group of men in black silhouette following me.

The panic I often felt when in situations I had no control over was getting worse and the pressure to keep a lid on it and not let anyone guess what was going on only added to my anxiety, especially when I started comprehensive school. The older I grew the more I just wanted to retreat into myself. My anxieties were crippling my confidence and I had stopped feeling like a carefree kid back when I was nine. Now my life was mostly all about getting through as best as I could.

Mr. Davies was tapping his watch and reminding me to hurry up. As fast as I could I wrapped my coat around me and pulled my clothes off from underneath, yanking my shirt out from the end one of the arm-holes. I kept hold of the coat with one hand and dropped my trousers. Then I quickly put my rugby shorts on, let my coat fall to the floor and tied up the laces on my boots. I felt the anxiety let go of me a little. It was over.

A few of the boys had been watching my performance. "What a sissy!" they jeered, but I ignored them and ran past, out onto the playing field with the other kids from my rugby class. Being skinny I was never any good at any sport and I spent most of the lesson frantically waving at kids walking past, on their way to lessons, or singing loudly. I knew the lyrics to countless songs from musicals.

"Wake up, Sheppard!" yelled Mr. Davies as the rugby ball zoomed past. He came marching over to me and stopped, shaking me by the collar of my top. "Don't just stand there, boy! Get a move on!" He pushed me towards the centre of the field where the other boys were in a scrum. I reluctantly joined in.

Afterwards we were told to get in the showers. If it wasn't bad enough being naked in front of boys my own age it was horrifying when thirty-something Mr Davies stood there in his tight shorts and bushy beard barking orders at us: "Use the soap!", "Scrub yourself properly, boy!" and "Dry yourself off!"

Although my school attendance record had never been perfect before, I began to play truant on games days. The duck pond became my second home. Soon I was spending every Tuesday and Thursday there, fishing and sharing my packed lunch with the ducks. Often Mondays were added to the Tuesdays and Thursdays and so it went on. I'd say goodbye to my family in the mornings, carrying my school bag with my packed lunch in, but I would slope off in the opposite direction towards the park. Sometimes Paul would skive off with me, but usually I was alone, thinking about how to get out of going to Frank's and how I was going to keep up with the excuses that would enable me to avoid games at school if I did have to go back. I was under so much pressure. The teachers were on to me and during the times I did attend classes they would ask where I had been the day before.

"I was ill," I told Mr. Davies when he cornered me at registration one morning. Unfortunately he was my class tutor as well as the games master.

"Well I need a letter of proof from your mother then, Ron," he said.

That evening I shut myself in my bedroom to think. I practiced my mother's signature over and over again on a piece of paper. I was sure that Mr Davies was about to turn up on the doorstep and ask my parents what was going on. I had visions of the police taking me down the station for questioning about my school attendance. Would they also grill me to find out about what I was doing with Frank?

I racked my brain for ideas. I had to come up with a good plan, and quickly.

5

It was a Wednesday night and the next morning I had cross country, which Mr. Davies had warned me that I had to go to as I had missed enough games lessons. I was lying in bed and Scruff was licking my hand and staring lovingly at me. His big eyes glistened through his shaggy fringe.

"What am I going to do?" I asked him and stroked his head. Scruff washed my face with his tongue.

I had told the teachers that I suffered from asthma and adopted a wheeze but it hadn't washed. I was reminded that unless I brought them a letter from my mother to prove I suffered from the condition that I had to go to all games classes from now on – no more excuses. I decided that I would go for a while, to get the teachers off my back, and I would come up with a plan in the meantime. All I had to do was to get through the following week at most. Feeling a little easier, I must have fallen asleep sometime in the early hours.

The next morning Mum gave me my packed lunch, which had bread and jam in it, and I sauntered to school with my games kit in my bag. I don't think I could have been walking very quickly because I missed registration and when I made my way into the changing rooms to get ready for cross country all the other boys were in shorts and T-shirts.

"Where have you been?" shouted Mr. Davies. It seemed to me that I could never get away from this fella. His moustache twitched with irritation.

"I don't feel well, sir," I wheezed and clutched at my throat. "I almost fainted on the way here."

"Don't you start that, Sheppard! Get changed!"

The other kids were looking at me and smirking.

"What you lot looking at?" I said.

"You lot – outside!" yelled Mr Davies, ushering the whole class towards the door. "Ron, you've got one minute! Hurry up!"

I quickly changed into my cross country kit and caught up with the others. It was a freezing cold November morning and I could see my breath on the air. Mr Davies took us through a few warm-up exercises and told us that today we would be doing two laps of the playing field, which I guessed was probably about five acres. I hated running even more than rugby or maths and as 30 other kids and I set off in the direction of the far-away trees on the other side of the field, where we were to run two wide-reaching circles of the entire grounds, I was already hatching a plan to get out of doing the whole distance.

I slowed down and let the other boys run ahead of me, so that they were at least a half a kilometre in front and I turned to see if I was out of Davies' eye-line. He was nowhere to be seen so I quickly darted across the school grounds and hid behind one of the classrooms on the outer edge of the playing field, where I sat for a few minutes. I peeked into the window and saw that it was a woodwork class, where kids were fashioning kitchen spatulas out of MDF. I sank down under the window and waited. The last thing I wanted was for a teacher to spot me and tell me off.

My legs began to turn blue and my teeth were chattering. After about five minutes I came out of my hiding place and blinked into the distance. I could see a line of boys in shorts trudging through the deep mud that was always at the bottom end of the playing field. There was still no sign of Mr Davies. I ran as fast as I could to the sports block and scaled around the back of the building and sprinted like mad towards the end part of the running circuit, which was also the same place as the starting line. I picked up a handful of mud and smeared it down my legs and slowly limped my way back towards the sports block again, hoping that Mr Davies would come out and spot me, assuming I had completed the first lap of the field. He did.

"What are you doing here?" he demanded.

"I managed one whole circuit, sir, but my asthma is bad."

"You mean you've already run a whole lap?" His face showed suspicion.

"Yes, sir, but I can't... breathe... I feel..." I began wheezing harder and clutching at my chest.

"OK, go and get showered then," he said. "You better not be messing me around, Ron," he warned.

"Yes, sir. I mean no... sir..." I stumbled my way over towards the changing rooms and was about to get changed into my uniform and dash to the duck pond when I heard a cough behind me. I turned. Mr Davies was standing behind me with his hands on his hips.

"What is it with you, Sheppard? Why do you never do as you're told? Showers, now!" he yelled and went to turn them on. I could hear the water hitting the white tiles and soon steam was inching its way out of the communal cubicle. "Now get undressed."

I looked around. There was only the two of us in the room. Although I knew that my teacher was no threat, I had a strong suspicion of all men, apart from my father. I had begun to hang out more with girls and tended to avoid too much contact with males. Girls were easier to talk to and most of my lunchtimes - when I did attend school - were spent with my friends, Loretta and Sharon. Loretta was a gentle quiet girl and Sharon was loud and chubby. We would eat our lunch and talk about music, films and anything else that took our interest. I still spent time with Paul and Geoff and my other mates, but avoided situations where I was surrounded by boys or men only. In an all-male changing room this was impossible, however. The thought of undressing in front of them was enough to make me stress out so much that there were times when I had had to hide in the toilets and change there.

Mr Davies was still glaring at me, so with trembling hands I took my shorts and top off and stood there in my vest and pants. Tears began to fill my eyes. I couldn't take the rest of my clothes off in front of a teacher, there was no way.

Luckily Mr. Davies' attention was elsewhere anyway and he could see that I was willing to do as I was told, so he left me to it. He warned me to wash myself properly and reminded me about the letter I needed from my parents if I was to be excused from cross country again. He then went to see what the other kids were up to.

As fast as I could, I dipped my arms and legs under the shower and dressed before anyone else came in the room and I dashed out of the school grounds to the duck pond. Maths was straight after cross country and I had had enough school for one day. I wanted to sit in the quiet and think about how I was going to get Mum to write a letter to Mr Davies. I pulled my coat closer around me, fished in my pocket for my woolly gloves and stayed in the park until it was the end of the school day. My parents didn't suspect a thing when I got home that afternoon.

"Good day at school, Ron?" asked my dad.

"Lovely thanks," I said.

Mum opened my bag and took my sports kit out to wash it. She was frowning.

"It doesn't look very dirty, Ron," she said, holding my shorts in the air.

"Wasn't very muddy today," I answered.

The next morning I went in to school and tracked down my friend Don at lunchtime. He had the neatest handwriting out of all my mates and I asked him to write a note to Mr Davies, pretending to be Mum, telling him that I did have asthma and should not have to do games any more. Don did just as I asked and signed the letter 'Winnifred Sheppard' in grown up writing and put my teacher's name on the front of the envelope. I then went to the staffroom, knocked on the door and handed the letter in, asking that it be given to Mr Davies. From then on I was excused from all sports at school. I was beside myself with happiness. Now I only played truant on days where we had maths. I couldn't think of a good enough excuse to get out of that as well.

In 1961, when I had just turned 13, I came home from the cinema, after seeing an old black and white movie with Lawrence Olivier in it, stood in the kitchen and announced, "I want to be an actor."

"That's nice," Mum said. She was bleaching out the bin and she didn't look up at me. My parents didn't take my singing and love of everything to do with entertainment seriously. No one in my area ever went into such a frivolous industry. Everyone became housewives, factory workers or worked for British Rail. My friend's dad was the foreman at the local abattoir. It made me sick to my stomach think about it. I wanted to do something different with my life.

My parents may not have taken my fancy aspirations seriously but they did their best to make sure that I got to enjoy my hobbies and would give me a few bob for an afternoon out here and there.

I loved 'Flash Gordon' and on my birthdays my parents would take me to see my favourite live act 'The Billy Cotton Live Band Show', sometimes followed by Cliff Richard and the Shadows. I had always loved movies and music but both became even more important to me after the abuse began. They helped me block out what was going on and offered me hope. This was crucial to my survival and sanity. I was determined that I would get out of this frightening situation – one day, when I was older. There was no way I was staying in an area that only reminded me of how bleak life could be. When I was singing or dreaming of the future it was the only time I felt like the old Ron again, the one before I hit nine and when Frank turned up. I was a good actor. To the outside world I was, on the whole, still daft Ron who liked a laugh. No one would have guessed that I had been going through hell every Sunday for four years by this time.

One Saturday morning my friends and I trotted off to the ABC Cinema in Kingston, where I had both my first sexual experience and my debut stage appearance. I was sitting in the back stalls on the balcony and a girl who occasionally hung around with me and my friends smiled and asked if she could sit in the seat next to me. Cassie had long blonde pigtails and was wearing a red dress and nail varnish. She was chewing bubble gum and making loud slurping noises with her lips. Paul, who was sitting on the other side of me, looked at her and elbowed me.

"She fancies you," he said.

"Nah, don't be daft." I liked girls but had no experience of anything remotely romantic.

"Yeah, she does. She's looking at you all funny," said Paul.

I glanced at Cassie who was facing straight ahead, blowing an enormous bubble.

"She was a minute ago," whispered Paul.

The lights went down and the credits of 'Flash Gordon' started to roll and about two minutes into the film I felt Cassie take my hand and shove it up her skirt. She didn't say anything or look at me, but carried on watching the big screen in front. I was embarrassed at first and didn't know what to do, but she was a confident girl for twelve years old and gently guided my hand down her knickers, urging me to move my fingers about a bit. She then took my hand out of her underwear, blew another big bubble and sauntered off.

My friends were sniggering at me and winking and although I felt silly I was proud that I'd had a fumble with one of the prettiest girls in town.

"You jammy sod, Ron," Geoff leaned towards me and whispered.

My grin almost split my face in two. "What can I say? Must be my charm!" I said.

When the film finished and the lights went up a man announced that there was a surprise for all the kids in the audience. There was a boy called Michael Cashman there, who had attended the local stage school and went on to win the lead role in 'Oliver' in the West End. Years later he starred in 'Eastenders'.

I was very excited and sat forward in my seat as he sang two songs from the show. The kids in the audience went mad afterwards, clapping and cheering. I was jealous and badly wanted to be in his shoes, so I left my seat and asked one of the staff if I could meet his manager – the one who had introduced Michael on stage. The audience had filed out by then but Paul and Geoff waited nearby for me. I was nervous but my determination to be an actor overtook any shyness and I walked up to a skinny bloke in a fancy suit and waistcoat.

The manager was called William Woods and he waved his arms about as if he were swatting wasps whenever he spoke. He asked me to sing something for him. I hadn't expected to audition on the spot. I gulped, looked at my friends who were nodding encouragingly at me and sang a few lines from 'Consider Yourself' from 'Oliver'. When I finished Paul and Geoff clapped.

"Very good, Ron," said Mr Woods and took me to one side. He went on to say that I had potential and that he wanted to meet my parents. I was ecstatic and after I told my friends I sprinted home as fast as I could.

I was out of breath and only managed to get half an explanatory sentence out, but my mother sat me down on the sofa and I eventually told my parents what had happened at the cinema. My family were very excited and spent the weekend cleaning the flat and preparing for Mr. Woods' arrival the following Monday. Mum and Nan even dusted the tops of wardrobes and doors.

Dad laughed. "We're not expecting the queen!"

"We don't want him thinking we're rough, like some of them around here," said Nan.

On the Monday at about four in the afternoon there was a knock on the door and Mum opened it. Mr. Woods smiled and sashayed in, wearing a suit and cravat. Waves of cologne wafted through the air.

"Well, *hello*," he drawled to my father in his posh voice and held out a hand for it to be shaken. Dad tentatively took his hand and gave it a light shake, before swiftly dropping it again. My parents and sister swapped surprised glances and weren't sure what to make of him. None of us had ever met a "proper theatrical" before – as my dad had labelled him. Dad sprayed cars for a living by this time and was covered in paint morning, noon and night, but today he had his best shirt and home-knitted tank top on.

Mum offered Mr Woods some tea and took his coat. He managed to find a comfortable spot on our lumpy sofa next to the cat, and put a hand out to stroke her. Ethel was getting on a bit and didn't suffer fools gladly, so she hissed, arched her back and sank her teeth into our visitor's hand. Mr. Woods screamed and sprang out of his seat.

"Oh dear!" he yelped.

Mum ran to him and inspected his hand. Luckily some of Ethel's teeth were missing so she hadn't injured him too badly.

"I'm so sorry, Mr Woods!" Mum said. "But there's no damage done."

"Are you sure?" He was visibly shaken.

I could see Dad, Nan and Pauline were trying not to laugh. Nan was pink in the face.

I recall thinking, *Oh bloody hell, let him give me a job and then make him go.*

Mr. Woods seemed to recover and took something out of his pocket. He then went over to our stereo player; put a cassette tape in and soon the first song from the musical 'Oliver' began to play. For a while he swayed a little and hummed under his breath, but he then slumped to his knees and began to wave his arms in the air, as if he were a conductor of an orchestra.

"Marvellous!" he kept saying and then he shouted when the music hit a crescendo: "Yes, that's it! Magnifico! Bravo!" His eyes were closed throughout and his hands wafted to and fro.

I looked at Mum and Dad, perching on their chairs, and mouthed to them: "please don't laugh", but I could see the edges of Dad's lips twitching. Mum had tears in her eyes and Nan's mouth was hanging open so widely I could see that her lower false teeth had risen upwards. Pauline was lying on her side on the sofa, holding her stomach from laughing so much.

Woods stopped all of a sudden, got up off his knees, turned the tape off and announced: "I'll need £300 to get Ron in a musical and I'll need the money now, so I can start on him straight away, take some professional photos and get him into stage school."

My parents couldn't afford that kind of money, so my mum thanked him and said that we'd be turning down his kind offer. In one way I was disappointed, but on the other hand I wasn't too bothered as I found William Woods odd and didn't want to be around him.

"What d'you reckon was up with him, Dad?" I asked after Woods left. "Bit weird, weren't he?"

"He's harmless, son. Just a bit limp-wristed like most theatricals," Dad answered and patted me on the shoulder.

"Oh, I see." I had no idea what he meant.

6

My asthma story was working very nicely with my teachers -until it was announced that the school was having an open evening and all the parents were sent invites. Mum and Dad were well aware that I sometimes bunked off in the past, but had no idea of how bad my school attendance had become.

There was no choice. I had to persuade Mum and Dad not to go. At age 12 I still received corporal punishment from my father occasionally, although I generally got a clip around the ear.

"I better not find out you've been bunking off again." Dad warned me when he opened the letter from the school. Unfortunately they didn't give us kids the invites to open evenings; otherwise I would have thrown it away, along with my school reports and anything else that I was meant to pass to my family.

The night of parent's evening Dad was in a bad mood with me and I could tell that I was getting on his nerves. He was red in the face.

"What's wrong with you, Ron? Will you let go of my jacket?"

"I don't feel well, Dad. Stay home with me – *please?*" I hung onto his lapels and tried to pull him backwards. He prized my hands off and told me to stop being so silly.

I put on a hacking cough and tried to look as pathetic as I could by shivering and wrapping my arms around myself. I leant on the table as if about to faint. Dad was in his best blazer and tank top and Mum had taken her curlers out to go and meet my teachers at school.

She wore a green Mac and matching eye-shadow and was rifling through her bag for her lipstick.

They were ignoring me. There had to be something I could do to stop them going. I let my knees buckle under me and as I crashed to the kitchen lino I clutched at my stomach.

"Ow!" I howled. "It hurts!"

"What is it now?" Mum sighed. "You just scoffed a huge piece of that pork pie Frank sent so I doubt there's much wrong with you... what do you think, Wally?" Mum looked at Dad.

"What about some castor oil? That should shift it," said Dad, smirking. He was doing his braces up and had an extra dollop of Brylcreem in his hair, which was slicked back flat to his head. His ears stuck out more than usual.

"No, no I'm sure it'll get better in a minute," I replied, jumping to my feet.

"Let's get you to bed. Pauline can get you anything you need while we're gone." Mum pulled me off the floor and led me to my bedroom.

"Why do you have to go out tonight, Mum? Stay in with me," I pleaded, hugging her arm.

"No, love. We need to speak to your teachers. See how you're doing at school. See you later. Be a good boy for your sister." She and Dad said goodbye and I heard the front door slam. Pauline had been listening to my performance and stuck her head in my bedroom door. She was laughing.

"Got something to hide, Ron? Been skiving off again?"

"Get stuffed, you!"

I jumped off my bed and ran a few steps towards her, but she ducked out of my way, cackling. I heard her speak as she walked back to the living room: "Such a thicko."

"Rotten cow," I mumbled.

Three hours later I heard the front door open and voices in the hallway. Mum and Dad were home. My bedroom door opened and let a slit of light in.

"Ron..." said Mum. "You awake?"

I squeezed my eyes shut and pretended to be asleep. I knew that I was in big trouble and I wanted to put off the inevitable for a little longer. The door closed and I was in darkness again. I sat up and put my bedside light on.

"Oh, bloody hell," I whispered to Scruff, who was panting dog breath in my face. "How am I going to get out of this one?" He licked me and put his paw on my hand, as he always did when I was upset.

The next morning I heard Dad call from the kitchen: "Ron, can we have a chat please?"

"I'm not well, Dad." I hid under the covers, hoping he'd believe me and go away. My stomach was doing aerobics. The next thing I knew Mum and Dad had stormed into my room and I was pulled out of bed in just my y-fronts.

"Don't you lie to me you cheeky little sod!" Dad slapped me on the leg. "Why haven't you been going to school?"

"But, I have, Dad!" I yelped.

He was pointing a finger at my nose and his eyebrows were practically touching. "You'll get another wallop! I'm warning you! And what's all this about asthma? You've never had asthma in your life!"

"What's asthma?" I asked.

"Ron!" Dad raised his hand as if to whack me again.

"Your teacher asked us how your condition was. We had no idea what he was talking about," Mum said, hands on hips. "Turns out I wrote a letter to the school on medical grounds, asking you to be excused because you have asthma. Funny that, considering I don't remember you having asthma or me writing such a letter!"

"It was *signed*!" Dad shouted. "Got one of your mates to do your mum's signature, did you?"

"I don't know what you mean, Dad," I said.

My father clamped hold of the front of my vest and pulled me so close to his face. "You're going to do as you're told for once and you're going to get your backside to school and if I catch you so much as being a minute late you'll be sorry!" Dad clipped me across the ear. I grabbed the side of my head which felt like it was vibrating. He then slapped my leg, so my other hand went to soothe the skin on my thigh.

"Ow!" I yelped.

"Do you understand?" He growled.

"Yes."

"Pardon?"

"I understand, Dad."

"Good, now stop playing silly buggers, get dressed and get to school!" He shouted and stormed out of the room.

Mum handed me my shirt and shorts. "Be a good boy, Ron. Everyone has to go to school. It's the law."

I pulled my clothes on and slouched my way in to class, dragging my bag along the ground. Mr Davies didn't say all that much, but he shadowed me like a stalker for the first few cross country classes I tuned up to.

When I had been playing rugby again for a few weeks it all became too much for me to bear. Sharing showers with 30 boys wasn't my idea of a pleasant experience. I began thinking of ways to get myself out of games without my parents finding out. It took me a while to concoct a cunning enough plan. By the time my 13th birthday came the following May, six months later, I was back to my old tricks. Instead of feigning illness I went to school with bandages on, having stopped off at the park on the way to wrap the white material around an arm or leg. The teachers probably knew I was making up excuses, but by then they had had enough of me. From then until I left school I think I 'broke' every bone in my body.

As I got into my teen years it slowly dawned on me that what Frank was doing to me was terribly wrong. I always felt that the abuse was disgusting and abnormal but I could never explain to myself exactly why. I was too young. I just knew that men and boys didn't act like that with one another.

By the time I reached 13 or 14 my interest in girls grew. My hate and anger towards my abuser intensified though I always I kept it hidden for fear of what he would do if I refused to let him do what he wanted. But I could sense that something inside me was changing and I wasn't sure how much longer I could take the abuse. If I could have got away with it I think I would have killed Frank. I fantasised about sticking a knife in him or smashing him over the head with something heavy.

In comparison, I saw that girls were soft and pretty; they had gentle hands and smelled nice. They were friendly and kind to me. They laughed at my corny jokes and liked my company. Girls didn't want anything from me. Sharon and Loretta were part of my gang at school but they also lived in the same block of flats as me and we'd spend hours playing songs on the gramophone my dad bought me for my 12th birthday. The first record I ever bought was Frank Ifield's 'I Remember You' and the three of us must have sung along to that in my room hundreds of times. The girls were always at my place. There was nothing frightening or intimidating about them and I felt safe around females. In their company the world was a far gentler and nicer place.

Frank, on the other hand, smelt of aftershave and mothballs. His starched shirts scraped across my bare skin as he stripped me naked and fondled me. Frank grew fatter and fatter the older he got and I particularly hated his hairy hands and his deep voice that barked at me to keep still and to stop crying. That voice was in my dreams most nights. When I woke in a sweat the suffocating darkness in my room offered me nothing but more terror. I began to sleep with the light on. When my dad complained about the electric bill I stayed awake under the covers with a torch and turn my lamp back on when my parents went to bed. Marlon and Scruff were always wedged in either side of me.

My parents got Scruff when I was just over a year old so by the time I was in my early teens he was pretty long in the tooth, but I had never thought about a time when he wouldn't be there. However, I noticed that he had stopped chasing me around and barking excitedly, wanting to play. He seemed tired and listless. He still slept with me on my bed and I would cuddle him until I fell asleep but his brown eyes looked cloudy and distant. Instead of licking me and jumping up and down when I came home from school one day he was laying on the sofa with his eyes closed. Mum was holding his paw and Dad put his hand on my shoulder.

"Scruff isn't well, Ron. We have to take him to the vet."

"He'll be OK though won't he, Dad?" I knelt down by Scruff and stroked him. His eyes opened and I pushed his bushy eyebrows off his face and kissed him. He blinked at me for a few more moments and closed his eyes again. I saw his chest heave with a sigh.

"I'm sorry, son. He is old," said Dad.

Mum had tears in her eyes when she explained that it would be kinder if they took him to be put to sleep if that's what the vet advised - and that Scruff had had a good life and loved me very much. She told me to be a brave boy, but it was too much for me to bear and I burst into tears, howling that Scruff was my best friend and that I didn't want him to go. But I could see that he was failing fast. Even his fur didn't look the same and his breathing was shallow. It seemed to me that he hadn't been himself for a month or so, although I had refused to believe that he was going to die soon. My parents had gently warned me as much and I chose to ignore them and hope for the best. But I could see that Mum and Dad were right.

Eventually I hugged and kissed my lovely dog goodbye and my parents took him to the vet, where he was put to sleep. I was in too much of a state to go with them so I stayed at home and said a prayer for him. I cried every day for two months. My parents thought I was just a sensitive kid who missed his dog, but Scruff really was my best friend. Just seeing his face and feeling the warmth of his body next to me in bed had got me through many panic-filled nights and when I woke from a nightmare he was always there with a lick on my face. I loved him more than anything. When he went I felt so lonely I didn't know if I could go on.

Soon after, my nan died of old age too and although I was never close to her I knew that she was about to leave us so I visited her in Kingston Hospital. She wasn't really all that coherent, but I put some flowers in a vase next to her bed and sat and chatted to her for a few minutes. She had only been in hospital for a few weeks, so I was shocked at how old and small she looked now; her skin was pure white and her bright pink nightdress stood out against her colourless complexion. I think she smiled at me while I twittered on about something or other for ten minutes, staring at the ill people in the beds in the ward. It was a scary place and the sight of drips and machinery gave me the creeps.

I touched her tiny hand, said "see you soon, Nan" and I left. I was the last person to see her alive. She passed away before any of the family could make visiting time. My sister and Mum were beside themselves with grief. Dad shrugged and said that she had had a "good innings".

At the funeral I said a prayer for Nan and asked her to find Scruff and look after him. She hadn't liked him all that much when he was alive but I thought that because he was now in spirit he would be less likely to lick her and wouldn't smell as bad. Nan said that his breath was disgusting.

The deaths left me with an even bigger sense of bleakness that I couldn't explain, even to myself, at that age. One of the worst aspects of my predicament with Frank was the crippling anxiety that had blighted my life since the first night it began and the terrible sensation of being detached from the world and the people in it. Today doctors would probably label it as depression. The feeling followed me wherever I went and sometimes subsided when I was in my room or at the pond where I felt that no one could find me. I was often surrounded by family and friends and that helped deaden the torment of the abuse too, particularly when we were mucking about and being silly. They were the times I loved the most when I was growing up. I lived for the lighter moments with my friends when we played pranks and ran amok. The times when we got caught smoking in Richmond Park by one of the other boys' parents, the afternoons we got kicked out of the local record shop for going up and down in the lifts, shouting and making a din. I even enjoyed the times I fought with my sister before she left home.

Mostly though I felt alone in the world and it was hard to cope with, especially when I didn't have Scruff's daft face to come home to any more.

7

After my fumble with Cassie at the cinema my general appreciation of girls turned into an adolescent admiration of another kind. At 14 I began to notice just how physically appealing they were.

Paul and I were sitting on a bench on the edge of the playing field one lunch time and we saw a group of older boys we knew laughing and shrieking over a magazine. Gary, a kid with an impressive crop of acne and a reputation for being a tough nut, snatched the magazine off another kid called Brian and they chased one another, jostling and running in our direction. Brian was waving the magazine in the air above his head.

"Give it back you bastard!" Gary shouted. He snatched it off his friend and the four boys all stopped again and began leafing through the pages. One of them shouted, "Cor blimey, look at the tits on that!"

"Hey Ron, want a look? Ever seen a pair of knockers before?" asked Brian, who sported an upturned shirt collar and greasy quiff.

"What you on about?" I asked and walked towards the gang, doing my best to look nonchalant.

"Course he ain't!" laughed Gary. "I bet he ain't never seen a girl naked before. He hasn't grown nuts yet."

"I've got nuts!" I said, affronted.

"What you all gawping at?" asked Paul, following closely behind me. His chin hit the ground when he saw what the other kids were making such a fuss about. We both stood and stared at the image on the pages of the magazine.

"Blimey," whispered Paul. "She's a big girl."

On the centre-spread was a topless blonde in a pair of skimpy briefs. I had never seen an almost naked lady before apart from the time I accidentally walked in on my mum in the bathroom – in her petticoat and pop socks. But this was much different. This girl was hot. My face went warm as I felt a twitch in my underwear.

"Bloody hell," I said. "Where d'you find that?" I asked, looking over my shoulder to check that none of the teachers were lurking about.

"Got it from my dad's shed," shrugged Gary. "He's got loads of 'em."

"Now we know what your dad does all day in that shed!" laughed one of the other boys in the gang.

"Can you blame him? You seen the state of Gary's mum?" shrieked Brian.

"Piss off!" Gary punched his friend in the arm. He practically pushed the magazine in my face. "Nice tits she's got eh, Ron?"

"They're all right," I shrugged, not knowing where to look or what to say. But I was speechless for another reason. The situation had a weird reassuring effect on my adolescent psyche. Maybe lusting over naughty pictures in the playground was a bit rude, I thought, but it meant that I was normal, like these other lads.

"Look, he's drooling all over her tits!" jeered Brian, bringing me back to the present. "Bet you'd like to shag her, wouldn't you, Ron?" Brian pronged me with an elbow and Paul and the rest of the group burst out laughing. I had no idea what "shag" meant although I had heard the word in the playground before. I looked at Paul. His face was blank too. We discussed girls and kissing and touching them, but our knowledge of sex was limited. I felt stupid.

One of the older boys elbowed me again. "Bet you'd like to give her a good shagging, wouldn't you, spindly legs?"

"Don't call me that... but yeah... I wouldn't mind..." I stammered.

"Wouldn't mind what, *spindly legs*?" jeered Gary.

"*I'd* like to give her a good shagging!" Paul's hand suddenly shot up in the air like he was answering a question in class.

"Would you, Paul? Know what to do with her would you?" Gary patted him on the head roughly.

"He wouldn't know where to put it," smirked Brian.

"Put what?" Paul asked.

The gang cackled and pointed at Paul, who turned red. I joined in ribbing my friend too, but in all honesty, I had no idea what the other boys were laughing at either. We then leafed through the rest of the magazine, looking at girls in their knickers, with the older kids discussing breast size and who would be the filthiest "shag". I assumed that they were talking about which girl washed the least.

It felt strange leering at naked girls in front of a group of older boys I hardly knew but I was glad that it happened. The banter and camaraderie made me feel normal. It was now clearer than ever that I fancied females and that what Frank was doing was plain wrong. Boys of my age, just like me, were keen on messing around with girls, not being touched by creepy old men.

I was faced with a big problem. How was I going to get away from Frank? I knew I couldn't carry on like this. I was dying inside.

It was Friday lunchtime and the next day Mum and Dad were taking me to Atherfield Bay, a holiday camp on the Isle of Wight. My sister had just married John and left home so I knew that my parents would spoil me and spend any spare money they did have on me. I was so beside myself with excitement that I packed my bag two weeks before we went. I began greasing my hair with Brylcreem, like Dad, fashioning it into a quiff, in case I met a girl there. I wanted to look manly. The anticipation of my first holiday, which I saw as "somewhere foreign" kept me awake for several nights before. Not only had I heard that they held bingo and talent contests but I was going to have a week's rest from Frank. I was determined to thoroughly enjoy myself, clear my head and think about how to rid myself of him once and for all when I returned.

Suddenly, I saw that my hands were shaking when I picked up my pen to write in my English lesson straight after the lunch break. The classroom wobbled before my eyes and I heard the teacher ask me if I was OK. I nodded, although I thought I was going to throw up. I bolted out of the room and ran to the toilets. I held on to the edge of one of the sinks and looked in the cracked mirror. Someone had written 'Mr Curry is a knob' on the wall next to it in red pen.

I took some deep breaths, washed my face in cold water and walked in the direction of the park. The excitement I felt about my holiday was still there but a question kept drilling at my brain. Did I have the guts to stand up to Frank?

8

Mum had recently had a hysterectomy so Dad said she deserved a break. He had heard somewhere that the Isle of Wight was to be the first place to open a holiday camp and considering he'd just been awarded £70 compensation for his back injury he thought he'd splash out. In the late summer of 1962 the three of us set out on the coach for the ferry that would take us to Atherfield Bay holiday camp.

The place was busy with tourists and the first thing I noticed was the swimming pool overflowing with kids laughing and screeching, some on inflatable rings and others jumping into the water from the side. Red coats stood around the paddling pool next to the main pool, shouting out encouragements to the smaller kids, who had to paddle through the waters balancing an egg on a spoon. Parents yelled their child's name, coaxing them on. Elvis Presley's 'Blue Hawaii' blasted out of a speaker in between loud announcements about that afternoon or evening's entertainment.

I followed my parents towards the reception area and on my way I peeped in a window and saw the ballroom. I noticed the stage and the lights – and the glitter ball hanging from the ceiling - and I was mesmerized at once. Red coats stood at one end chatting and blowing up balloons; the girls in pony-tails and thick make-up and the men in slicked back hair and crisp white plimsolls. I was only 14 but I decided that I wanted to be a red coat when I left school.

We and a few other families were given our room keys and each shown to our chalets, which were built from wood and stood in long lines. Dad pointed out the huge football pitch to one side of the camp and Mum was excited about the crazy golf area.

We unpacked our bags in the chalet, which had one bedroom for my parents and I was to sleep on a pull-out bed in the living area. The place had flowery curtains and bedspreads, pine furniture that matched and an en suite bathroom with a shower. At home we had to make do with a lukewarm bath each once a week so it all seemed very luxurious.

"It's lovely, eh, love?" My dad put his arm around my mum's shoulders.

"Wonderful." Mum carefully hung her best dress on a hanger and smiled. I could see the tension leave her face. It was nice to see her so relaxed and happy. I gave her a big hug.

"What's got into you two?" she laughed.

"Let's go to the pool!" I said. I quickly changed into my new trunks Mum had knitted especially for the trip in the living room area, draped a towel over my shoulder and waited for my parents to get ready. Dad came out of the bedroom in a pair of baggy knee length shorts and his string vest and Mum wore a flowery swimming costume with a matching short skirt.

"You look smashing, Win!" Dad said. "C'mon then, let's go!"

We found some deckchairs that edged the pool and as Mum and Dad reclined with a beer they bought from the nearby bar, I, being a non-swimmer, enjoyed a doggy paddle while hanging on to the side of the pool and joined in with a few other kids, knocking a blow up ball about. The weather was glorious and as I looked around me all I could see were smiles. It was only my first day and I didn't want to think about how I was going to tackle Frank yet. I just wanted to enjoy being a typical boy for a while, to feel like the other kids in the camp did.

I fancied an ice-cream so I went to pull myself up the small metal ladder attached to the side of the pool, but the water clung to the thick wool of my swimming trunks, weighing them down as I pulled myself skywards. I could feel my bare bottom peeping out at everyone. I let go of the bars on the side of the ladder and got back under the water.

Has anyone seen my arse? I wondered. Without looking around I put one hand on the back of my trunks to secure them in place, hauled myself out of the water and ran and sat in the deckchair next to Mum. I looked at the ground, my face burning. I was sure I had heard sniggers.

"What's wrong, love?" Mum asked.

"Nothing." I lived in my light cotton shorts from then on.

That evening Mum put her best dress on and even wore lipstick and earrings and we made our way to the dinner hall for our evening meal of chicken, chips and peas. Afterwards we went into the ballroom and took seats in the second row. The evening's entertainment was about to begin and I couldn't wait. Three men in sequined jackets and bow ties sang popular songs from the radio and reeled off a list of jokes which made the audience roar with laughter. But the one that stood out for me was an entertainer called Ray Baraclough, who later went on to work with Les Dawson and to play Alec on 'Coronation Street'. I cornered him after the show, asking him how I could get a job in a holiday camp like him.

"How old are you?" Roy asked me.

"14. How old do I have to be?"

"At least 18. So what can you do? Can you sing? Do impressions? Dance?" he said.

"I can do anything, me – you name it!"

Roy laughed and he told me there was a talent contest later in the week which I should enter. I was chuffed. A real entertainer was showing an interest in me. Roy came over to meet my parents who were having a drink at one of the tables in the ballroom and introduced himself. We saw him often that week and he was always full of smiles and advice for me about show business, even though he must have been in his early to mid 20s and I was just a skinny little kid.

The second night of my holiday was probably the best for me. I met a girl. Her name was Lesley and she was slim and pretty with dark hair cut in a fashionable 60s style. My parents sat at the table next to her mum and dad in the bingo hall and they got talking, so while they nattered on about the game Lesley and I butted in and said that we wanted to go for a walk on the beach nearby. When we got to the edge of the holiday camp we found that we had to walk about what looked like hundreds of steps to the beach and as Lesley admired the beautiful sea view I thought, *bloody hell, how are we going to get back up all them?*

Lesley and I sauntered down the steps in the darkness, listening to the sea swish in the background. I could see the lights of a town twinkling in the distance and I thought how romantic it was.

"Parents are so boring, liking bingo, aren't they?" I sighed. "It's all so old hat."

"So embarrassing!" Lesley grimaced.

"You wait; you haven't seen my dad with a knotted hanky on his head yet…" I said.

"He doesn't wear that, surely!" Lesley grimaced again.

"He does – and a string vest. He gets sunburn through the holes."

"You should see my dad dance," said Lesley.

"No you should see mine – it's like this." I stopped on a step for a moment and mimicked my father dancing, which reminded me of a drunk heading out of the pub after 10 pints; his legs buckling all over the place. Lesley giggled and I was pleased that I had made a pretty girl laugh.

We joked some more and bonded over our shared embarrassment of our families while we threw stones in the sea. I caught a few glimpses of Lesley's profile in the dimness of the night as she spoke and thought how good looking she was. I wanted to stay on that beach forever. It had been a long time since I felt so carefree. Although I fancied Lesley and was keen to kiss her it was our first 'date' and I didn't make a move on her. Walking up the steps, back to the bingo hall, I took her hand and we smiled at one another.

During the bingo game both our parents' had arranged to go on a trip the next day so Lesley and I were overjoyed that we would be seeing one another so soon. Lying in bed I couldn't wait for the next day to begin. It was the first night in ages that I didn't dream about Frank or the dark monsters that dogged me.

As we all walked along the beach at Alum Bay the following morning the sun was out and so were people in skimpy bathing costumes. When I spotted a woman of about 20 stone in a bathing suit I did a waddling walk behind her while Lesley shrieked with laughter. Egged on, I then spotted a male jogger in skimpy swimming trunks that left little to the imagination, so I did a silly run behind him, flicking my legs out at the sides, covering my crotch area with both hands. Lesley fell about laughing.

"What are you doing, Ron?" Dad asked, making me stop what I was doing. He was a few metres in front, talking with the rest of the adults.

"Nothing, just chatting," I said.

"Stop taking the mickey out of people."

"Yes, Dad," I said.

I waited until he turned back to his conversation with the others and sidled up behind him, mimicking his walk and jutting my head backwards and forwards. I scratched my head like a chimpanzee and turned to look at Lesley, crossing my eyes and pushing my bottom jaw forward as far as it would go so I had a dramatic overbite. I didn't realize that Dad had turned to watch what I was doing; not until I felt a sharp clout on top of the head, followed by: "I told you to pack it in you little git!"

"Sorry, Dad," I said and slunk back to Lesley, who was holding her hand to her mouth and giggling.

That evening the adults went to bingo again and Lesley and I made our excuses and headed down to the beach, this time with me holding her hand as we walked down the steps. When we got to the bottom Lesley told me not to let her hand go and we spotted a rock in a fairly dark area so we made our way to it and sat down. We looked at one another. I could tell that Lesley felt as nervous as I did. Our faces drew closer and we kissed. Our breathing grew heavier and our hands traveled up and down each other's bodies – until mine found their way onto Lesley's breasts, which I gently caressed. I couldn't believe my luck.

"We better get back. They'll be wondering where we are," Lesley said suddenly, pulling her clothes straight and standing up. She reached out for my hand and we went back to the bingo hall, where our parents were waiting.

"What time do you call this?" Lesley's dad said. "Bingo finished ten minutes ago."

"Where you been, Ron?" Dad was eyeing me suspiciously.

I hoped my face wasn't turning red. "We bumped into some other kids. Must have lost track of the time," I fibbed.

Both sets of parents nodded. We all agreed to meet the next evening.

Most days were spent by the pool and each night the adults played bingo and then enjoyed the entertainment in the ballroom. Lesley and I always sneaked off to the beach as soon as we could, knowing full well that each time we met our physical relationship would go a step further than the night before. We hadn't spoken about carrying on seeing each other when we got home; Lesley lived in Leicester and I was in Kingston, but I hoped that when I returned I would be able to tell my mates that I had a proper girlfriend.

The holiday proved to me that it was possible to be happy and that my one sole source of misery was Frank. I didn't want some dirty old man spoiling my life any more. But how was I going to get away from him? Would he leave me alone if I told him about Lesley, I considered? I sat in a deckchair by the pool licking an ice-cream and thoughts whizzed around my head until it hurt. Then something struck me; had I actually done anything wrong? Wasn't *Frank* the one being bad? And if that was so, why would *I* go to prison? There was so much to think about and I had no answers, but I was growing up and a streak of sensibility, and even rebellion, was breaking through my consciousness. Somehow I was sure that it was only a matter of time before I would have the courage to stand up to my abuser. I just didn't know how or when.

I made my way to the chalet where my parents were to get ready for the talent competition Roy Barraclough had encouraged me to enter. Butterflies gnawed at my stomach. It was Thursday night and I had to morph into Tommy Steele.

"Hurry up, Ron," Dad said when I walked into the chalet. "We need to get to the dinner hall and then it's your big stage debut."

After dinner we went to the ballroom and found a table near the front of the stage. I was so excited I thought I'd wet myself. The glitter ball rotated, throwing sparkles of light across the room. Mum had had her hair done and Dad was wearing a proper jacket with lapels. I went over the lines of my song in my head until the lights dipped and Roy came on stage to announce the beginning of the talent competition.

A little girl in a pink frilly dress was up first and she loudly whistled 'Over the Rainbow' through the gap in the front of her teeth. I began to laugh. Dad elbowed me and growled "stop it!" During the song Lesley sidled up to sit beside me and whispered that she hoped I would win. My nerves grew. I had persuaded myself that it could be my big chance, that someone might notice me and sign me up as an entertainer.

Next up on stage was two sequined nine-year-olds dancing the Samba. Roy then motioned towards me and I got up on stage next to him.

"Please welcome Ron Sheppard as Tommy Steele!" he announced. The band began to play the track and I stood at the microphone at the front of the stage. All eyes were on me. Dad stuck his thumb up. I could see Lesley smiling encouragingly. Then I began to sing: 'Little White Bull' I did the Tommy Steele voice and mannerisms and I could see people clapping along and others smiling. My voice had greatly improved since I was a little kid. I had spent many years perfecting my impression of my favourite star that after it was over the crowd cheered and Lesley told me how good I was. My parents said that they were proud of me. When Roy later announced that I had won and I had to go up on stage and accept my prize of vouchers to be spent in the holiday camp's shop I was the happiest kid on the planet. The night got even better when Lesley and I went to the beach again and we put our hands down each other's underpants.

On the last night Lesley and I went to a secluded spot on the beach again and kissing soon turned into touching and fumbling. She undid the zip on her trousers so I could touch her intimately and she then pulled down the zipper on my jeans. We were so overcome with lust that we had sex. I didn't tell Lesley it was my first time and she didn't say whether she had done it before either. It was over quickly, but we smiled at each other afterwards, happy that it had happened. We got dressed and then threw stones in the sea, talking about the holiday and what fun we had had. We agreed to keep in touch and hopefully meet up soon. I was sad as we walked up the beach steps for the last time. The week was over and the next day I would be going back to my normal life. A lump formed in my throat and I gently squeezed Lesley's hand. I wished I could take her with me.

On the coach on the way back to Kingston I stared out of the window in the seat behind Mum and Dad and thought of the wonderful week I had just had. I remembered Lesley's laugh and the way she smelled of shampoo and how soft her lips were when I kissed her. But that feeling of bleakness I was used to was creeping back in. We were now on UK soil and edging closer to home. That meant I was nearer to *him*. It was Saturday evening and there had been no mention of my seeing Frank the next day, as I usually did. As we had been on holiday he hadn't been able to contact us. A warm glow had enveloped me and kept me safe all week. The Isle of Wight became a symbol of freedom and contentment for me for many years after. All I had to do was to see the place mentioned on TV or pictured on a tea towel and I would become a little teary.

I assumed that because there had been no mention of a Sunday outing with Frank that I was off the hook. I could hardly breathe as I leant around the seat to speak to Dad.

"Can I go out with my mates tomorrow?"

"Course you can," nodded Dad.

I placed my head against the coach's window and drifted off to sleep, thinking about losing my virginity to Lesley.

The next morning I couldn't wait to tell my friends all about my news and I practically sprinted around to Loretta's flat which was two floors down in the same block. Sharon was already there and we walked to the park and met Paul, Geoff and Steve on the way. We sat down by the duck pond, where I told them about winning the contest and Lesley.

"Did you do it then, Ron?" asked Paul.

I smiled but kept quiet.

"He's not going to tell *you*," laughed Loretta, flicking her long auburn hair off her face.

"Let's just say that we didn't just hold hands," I said.

Steve leaned forward and looked at me. "Really?"

"You lucky git," Paul whined. "It's not fair; I'm never going to get a girlfriend."

"Maybe you would if you changed your socks once in a while," said Sharon.

"My feet don't smell." Paul yanked his foot up to his nose and took a good sniff of his plimsoll. He frowned. "Oh."

"Exactly," said Sharon.

We knew it was teatime, when our parents expected us to be home, because Paul's stomach began to growl loudly. So the boys went off in the direction of home and Loretta, Sharon and I sauntered towards the flats. I was smiling and singing 'Little White Bull' when I walked into the kitchen. Mum was back in her hairnet, cleaning the cooker.

"What's for tea, Mum?" I asked.

"You're going out for your tea," she beamed.

"Great. Where we going?"

Dad was at the table. "Frank's coming to pick you up. He called and wants to take you to a nice café in Richmond."

I felt as if someone had punched me in the stomach.

"But, Dad…"

"Quickly now; go and have a wash and put a clean t-shirt on," Mum said.

"But, Mum… I don't…"

"Stop dithering and hurry up. He'll be here in ten minutes!"

She ushered me out of the kitchen and into the bathroom and shut the door behind me. "Don't forget to wash behind your ears. You don't want Frank thinking you're dirty," she called.

I sat on the edge of the bath and wept.

9

That night I got home from Frank's and announced that I was going straight to bed. Mum was drinking her nightly pint bottle of Guinness and sewing socks, while Dad was at the pub with his mates. He went to the local pub about three times a week and Mum was forever dumping his dinner in the bin because it had gone stone cold when he didn't return home on time.

"You alright, Ron?" she asked. "It's not like you to go to bed this early. You're not coming down with something are you? You spent a lot of the holiday in that pool."

I shook my head. "I'm alright. Just tired."

"Did you have a nice time with Frank?"

"It was fine, Mum. Night." As I walked to my room and got undressed I could still feel his hands on my bare skin and I was dying to have a wash and read my comics in bed. The £5 reward he gave me fell out of my jeans pocket and floated to the floor. I always spent the money on football cards or sweets. I thought it was the least I deserved, considering what I had to endure. Although I had promised myself before I went to the Isle of Wight that I would spend the holiday thinking of ways to get Frank out of my life all I had done while there was block him out of my mind as much as I could and have fun. Now it was back to the stark reality of life and I had been thrust back into the recurring nightmare of sexual abuse again. I felt hopeless.

After a quick wash, I lay on my bed hugging my knees to my chest and sobbed quietly so that Mum wouldn't hear me and come to see what was wrong. Over and over I asked myself "why me?" I couldn't see an end to it.

Dudley had been on one side of Frank in the cinema and I was seated on the other. Sometime during the film I felt Frank's hand rubbing my thigh and I moved my leg away from him, inching my whole body as far from his person as I could manage in such a confined space. But I couldn't concentrate on the movie and have no recollection of what was playing that night. I was too busy dreading what was going to happen once the credits rolled and we got to Frank's place.

Later, after he dropped Dudley off at his house, which wasn't too far from where I lived, Frank took me into his front room and performed sex acts on me, as usual. And now, as I lay in bed, thinking of my wonderful holiday, it seemed like a false memory. It was too good to be true. A hazy image of Lesley and her soft skin played on my mind; I pictured us holding hands on the beach, kissing and having sex for the first time. Lesley had finally proven to me that I was a normal lad and it felt so wonderful to know that about myself.

When she called me a few weeks later and told me she had a boyfriend I was a little upset but we lived miles apart and I was just happy that I had had the experience. It made me feel like I was growing up, into a man, and that soon I would be even stronger and able to do something about Frank. I prayed for that day to come soon.

Something else began to niggle at the back of my mind, morning, noon and night. The holiday had shown me that there was a lot more out there in this world than Kingston, the depressing block of flats where I lived and school. I began to hope that I would escape and become an entertainer. I may not have been the cleverest kid in the world but I could sing and people found me funny. I was determined I was going to be on the stage in one form or another. Atherfield Bay holiday camp and meeting Roy Baraclough and Lesley had given me belief in myself, something I lacked before. Still, to this day, I think of them both often and give them credit for changing the way I felt about life and me as a person.

I was even more determined to get through my last 18 months of school and to leave Kingston far behind. I bunked off from my lessons as much as I could get away with, practiced my Tommy Steele routines in my bedroom and counted down the days until I was out of there.

In May 1963 I was 15 and it was a few months after my birthday when my parents gave me some news. We were sitting at the kitchen table, eating a meal Mum had made from the ingredients from one of Frank's food parcels, when Dad said: "How d'you fancy going to Benidorm, son?"

"Where's that?"

"Spain," said Dad.

I couldn't believe my ears. My parents were always skint and I had never been somewhere so exotic before. I considered the Isle of Wight to be abroad, but Spain; it was the same as Barbados as far as I was concerned. I immediately had images of exotic girls in bikinis, wearing hula shirts and flower garlands, in my head.

"Blimey, Dad! Spain! Yes, please!" I spluttered and breathed a pea back down into my throat, making me cough and choke.

"Be careful, love." Mum smacked me on the back. "It's kind of Frank, isn't it?"

I felt my face flush and I coughed even more. "What?"

"Frank's booked a week's holiday in Benidorm in September and he's taking you!" Dad eyes were almost popping out of his head. "Isn't that exciting?"

I stopped coughing and put my knife and fork down with a clank. I felt like yelling "No! He's a disgusting old pervert who keeps touching me! Please, Mum, Dad, don't make me go!" But I couldn't say anything. I could hardly breathe, let alone speak. The walls and floors closed in around me and I felt sick and dizzy. Tears welled in my eyes and I had to bite my lip to stop myself from slumping forward onto the table and bawling my heart out. This couldn't be happening to me.

My parents laughed at my reaction, thinking I was speechless and emotional with surprise and they began talking about all the things I would be doing on holiday. I listened to them chatter on about the sea, the beach, the hot weather and the posh hotel we would be staying in, but I knew damn well why Frank wanted to take me away with him. It wouldn't be a fun and carefree holiday. I would be his captive, his sex slave, and I was going to have a whole week of him molesting me, with no distractions. It was only July and I now had two months of hell, dreading what was in store for me. I would be far away from everything and everyone I knew, in a foreign country with Frank.

In the weeks that followed I began hoping that he would drop dead before I had to set foot on the plane. Images of accidents with double decker buses, as Frank was crossing the road, played on my mind like a scene from a movie. I told myself that because he was fat he ate too much and it was a strain on his heart. I hoped that he would eat even more, until he was fit to burst, and keel over. But luck wasn't on my side. On September 10th Frank, Dudley and I headed for Heathrow Airport. I had no idea that Dudley was coming along but he was a quiet 18-year-old and gave me the impression that he couldn't be bothered with me, so as I sat in the back of Frank's car, Dudley and Frank ignored me and chattered excitedly about the forthcoming wonders of the Costa Blanca. I didn't like Dudley much but I was glad he was there to distract Frank.

I hoped that the car would crash, killing Frank but only maiming me slightly so I was well enough to be let out of hospital and return home, but that wish didn't come true either. It struck me that I didn't ask for much and although I knew it was wrong to pray for such things to happen to people I didn't feel guilty about it or worry that I would go to Hell because I had good reason and I was sure that God would understand.

I'd never been on an aeroplane before and once I had got over my initial nerves I loved every minute of the flight. Frank sat in between Dudley and me, sipping brandy, and I was in the aisle seat.

When we got to the 4-star hotel I was speechless and Dudley said: "Shut your gob or you'll catch a fly." The place looked like a palace, what with the marble floors and the mosaics on the walls of the huge lobby area. Staff in extravagant blue and gold uniforms, which reminded me of pantomime costumes, flitted about with cases, trolleys and clipboards, in between masses of holidaymakers checking in or leaving for the beach.

I noticed that some people were speaking English, but there was another language mixed in between and I couldn't work out what people were saying.

I nudged Dudley: "Why's everyone speaking in a foreign language?" I asked.

He snorted. "Because we're in Spain you stupid pillock."

We were ushered to the lifts by one of the staff and as we made our way to the 10th floor I looked around me. "Where's our cases?" I shrieked.

"*God, Ron,*" Dudley sighed as his eyeballs rolled upwards. "The hotel porter will bring them up separately. Don't you know *anything*?"

Since I hit about 11 I had had the suspicion that Dudley was another of Frank's playthings, but even knowing that, I didn't particularly warm to him and I couldn't work their relationship out. Dudley seemed to look up to Frank and would often show off in front of him, which would sometimes involve making me look stupid. I didn't care; I didn't want Frank's attention. I told myself to enjoy the holiday as best as I could and to try and keep out of Frank's way. I hoped that he would be more interested in the older boy than me. But I suspected he would find enough time for both of us. From the moment we stepped into the hotel lobby I don't think Frank's smile left his face once during the whole week.

10

I was relieved to find out that we had a room each with our own keys, situated next to one other, with Frank's room being in the middle of mine and Dudley's. I left the other two to it and made my way into my room which was furnished with a comfy sofa, a double bed and a fridge. I then walked out onto the balcony, which overlooked a gorgeous sandy beach. As I stood there with the sun on my face and palm trees swaying around the hotel grounds I thought it was an idyllic setting, but I hated being there. I wanted to go home. The sight of the double bed sent shivers down my spine.

There was a knock at the door and the porter brought my luggage in. I changed into cotton shorts and a t-shirt and waited for the others to come and get me. Frank had said that we were heading down to the pool area. A few moments later there was a tap at the door and I went and opened it. Frank and Dudley were standing there. Dudley's long skinny legs poked out of baggy shorts and Frank was grinning from ear to ear, wearing tight trunks and a short-sleeved shirt. His gut strained against the material, as if he was nine months pregnant and his sweaty bald head gleamed through his comb-over. I was revolted.

"Right, boys!" Frank said and rubbed his hands together. "Let's go to the pool! I could do with a drink!"

I followed behind as we walked to the lift and on the way to the pool I sneered while Frank bragged about what lucky boys we were to be on such a lavish holiday with him and that the hotel was the top one in the area. He kept mentioning how much money he had spent on us, even as he bought cocktails for him and Dudley and a Coke for me. I wished I was old enough to drink alcohol. I would have drunk the bar dry.

We lay on sun-loungers by the pool and while my eyes bulged at the girls in bikinis, Frank and Dudley were deep in conversation as usual. I hardly ever listened to what they talked about but I picked up on Dudley saying something about the last time they had been to Spain together. I couldn't fathom why this lad got on so well with Frank and why he didn't seem to be disgusted by him. I had never seen him recoil from Frank when he put his arm around him or when he grabbed him by the shoulder. They were discussing having a game of tennis again, like the last time they had been away. I wondered about Dudley's parents and if they knew what Frank was up to. I doubted it. Frank was devious. He covered his tracks. He was the perfect predator. But still I couldn't fathom why Dudley enjoyed being with the man. Looking back on it I now realise that Frank Bush had spent ages grooming the kid. When I first met Dudley he was 13 so he would probably have known Frank for years. I assumed that Dudley came from a poor and unhappy background and perhaps he put up with Frank in order to escape his home life. He was painfully thin and pale, but then so was I, except he did look extremely unhealthy most of the time and his skin was covered in spots. While my family were poor I was close to my parents and I talked about them a lot. Dudley never once mentioned his personal life.

During the holiday Dudley would sometimes call him 'Uncle Frank' and again it crossed my mind that they could be related, but it seemed too warped to believe. Frank asked me to call him the same several times but gave up when I refused.

Frank unbuttoned his shirt, stood and stretched. The hairs on his belly caught the sunlight and his fat jiggled. I averted my eyes.

"Fancy a swim, boys?" he asked.

"OK." Dudley got up.

"Ron?" said Frank.

"No thanks. I'll stay here," I replied.

"C'mon!" Frank tried to grab my arm.

I pulled away. "No thanks. You two go."

"C'mon, Frank, let's go," said Dudley.

Frank grabbed my arm and yanked me to my feet.

"We're on holiday, Ron!" Frank grinned. "Have a swim with me!"

"I can't swim," I mumbled, feeling my face flush.

Dudley snorted. "You can't swim! What a sissy!"

"I'll teach you," said Frank, propelling me to the shallow end of the pool. "Go on, get in."

Reluctantly, I climbed down the pool ladder on the side and got into the water while I watched Dudley run and dive in the deep end and come to the surface, laughing and splashing about. Frank did a stretch, took a few breaths and his short fat legs launched him off the side and he did a belly flop into the pool which made a huge splat sound. After a few seconds he came up gasping for air, arms flailing, until he launched into a nonchalant breast stroke. I was giggling uncontrollably, clutching onto the edge of the pool. Dudley was doing energetic lengths and Frank made his way over to me.

"Let me teach you to swim, Ron," he said and held his arms out.

"No thanks, I'm fine here," I said.

Frank splashed forward and tried to grab me.

I pulled backwards. "No! I'm fine!"

Frank held onto my arm and put his hands under my stomach, forcing me into a swimming position. I wriggled under his grasp but he was a lot stronger than me.

"Now, Ron. Splash your legs and put the backs of your hands together in front of you and push the water out sideways."

I couldn't concentrate on what he was saying. All I was bothered about was that he had his hands on me, just above the waistband of my shorts and I didn't want them creeping any lower.

"I don't like it," I said and wriggled again. Frank held on to me.

"Go on! Try and swim!" he growled.

"I don't want to!" I shouted and struggled to stand up, sending splashes of water everywhere.

Frank quickly let me go and swam off towards Dudley.

"Go on then, sod off you pervert," I muttered. I watched as Frank and Dudley trod water and enjoyed a chat in the deep end. I stayed on my own in the pool for a couple of hours, until Frank came to get me and said that we were going to dinner. By then my face was burnt and my skin was wrinkled from the water.

We went back to our own rooms to get changed and met downstairs in the restaurant, a large room with marble flooring and tables covered with white linen cloths and silver cutlery. I had never been to such a posh place and looked at the waiter blankly when he asked what I wanted to order. Frank and Dudley had some kind of local dish but I didn't like anything new or fancy so I said I wanted burger and chips. I had seen the fish on other people's plates and noticed it didn't have batter on it so I wasn't taking any chances. Dudley's eyes rolled to the heavens when I asked for ketchup.

While the other two ate and talked Dudley had his index finger wedged up his left nostril and was having a good rummage around. I couldn't believe it, especially when Frank didn't say anything. If I had done that in front of my dad at the dinner table I would have got a clip around the ear and sent to bed.

Dudley pulled out whatever he had found up his nose, inspected it and shoved it in his mouth. I thought I was going to be sick.

"Would you like some salt with that?" I asked.

"What?" Dudley said, oblivious and carried on chatting to Frank as he wiped his hand on his shorts.

Afterwards we went to the lounge bar to watch the cabaret while Frank drank double brandies and Dudley tried different cocktails, decorated with fruit and umbrellas.

By midnight Frank was tipsy and keen to head back to his room, which I was glad about. It meant I could lock myself in and climb into bed. I assumed that if he was going to bother anyone it would be Dudley, but considering how many brandies he had consumed I felt it was more likely he would simply fall asleep as soon as his head hit the pillow. I was right. He left me alone and after lying awake for a few hours, worrying about Frank knocking at my door, I eventually drifted off. My nightmares that night were more disturbing than ever.

The following day and evening was pretty much like the one before, except Frank and Dudley had a few games of tennis in the hotel's courts. I wanted to be left alone by the pool but they insisted that I act as ball boy, running about after them in the sun. By the end of the day I was burnt and asked Frank if I could stay in my room, instead of going to dinner with the two of them. My skin wasn't all that sore but I put on a bit of a performance, hoping I could keep out of their way.

"Don't be daft. Put some lotion on and join us in the restaurant," said Frank on our way back up to our rooms. "You've got to eat."

Ten minutes later the three of us sat at our dining table, where I asked for chicken and chips, much to Dudley and Frank's disdain. Frank tried to get me to have a local dish, the same as him.

"I'm not eating fish with its head and fins still on," I said, crossing my arms. "And I want ketchup on my chips!" He gave up after that.

After we watched a flamenco act in the hotel lounge Frank announced it was time for bed and we all made our way back to our rooms. I feigned tiredness and without saying goodnight I locked my door and jumped into bed. Ten minutes later I heard a gentle tap at the door. I hid under my bedclothes and pretended to be asleep. My stomach was doing somersaults. There was another knock.

"Ron," I heard Frank whisper. "Ron…"

I put my pillow over my head and turned my body in the opposite direction. "Go away," I muttered. "Please leave me alone."

I heard a louder knock, followed by "Ron, Ron; wake up. It's me, Frank."

Again and again he tapped on the door. "Let me in, Ron. I know you're awake," he said loudly and banged once more.

"I'm tired, Frank," I called.

"Let me in!"

"I don't feel well. All the sun…"

"Ron, open the door!"

I knew then that Frank wasn't going anywhere. I had visions of him going down to reception for another key and if he did that he would be able to enter my room any time he wanted. He didn't seem to care who heard him in the hallway; he was determined. Eventually I got out of bed and went to the door. Tears filled my eyes as I let him in.

"Get back into bed, Ron," he said. I stood there, shaking with fear, not knowing what to do.

"Bed," he reminded me.

I climbed under the covers in my vest and pants and stared at the ceiling. Then I heard him remove his shirt and unzip his trousers and let them fall to the floor. Inside I was praying that he would leave me alone. I felt him approach me, pull the covers off and climb in next to me. He put his arm over the front of my body.

"What're you doing?" I asked, sitting bolt upright.

"I'm getting into bed with you," he said.

"No!"

"I want to sleep with you." Frank went to lay down.

"No, get out!" I knew he wanted full sex. He had tried to persuade me to go further with him before. The thought made me sick to the stomach. Frank looked at me and got out of bed, but it wasn't over. Reminding me that I was alone with him in a foreign country and that no one would believe or help me, he made me sit on the edge of the bed and he performed oral sex on me. When he was done he put his clothes back on and left my room and I stayed awake until the morning, crying. Every other night after that was the same. I could only assume that he was alternating between Dudley and me. Dudley seemed unperturbed by what was going on and spent most of the holiday in the pool or tennis court with Frank. We even wandered around old churches and a museum, which bored me rigid, and all the time Frank and Dudley acted like great pals without a care in the world.

Why does he think what he's doing is alright? I asked myself while Frank wandered around a gift shop in his flip-flops, browsing through postcards. *Doesn't he care that he's ruined my life?* But men like Frank never think that what they are doing is wrong.

Each day of that holiday I watched Frank in his swimming trunks, lying by the pool, his skin neon pink from all the sun on his massive belly, and I despised him. I was a 15-year-old kid and he was a grown up. He was a monster. I knew that if I didn't do something that I could be 18 like Dudley, going on holiday with Frank, being at his mercy. But I wasn't Dudley. Six years of abuse was enough.

On the last night of the holiday it was Dudley's turn to play host to Frank in his room and I lay awake most of the night. Over and over I thought: *Enough is enough.*

It was the morning of our return to the UK and I packed my case and went downstairs to meet the others for breakfast. Throughout the meal and the flight home I was silent, mulling over what I was going to do. *Enough is enough*, kept running through my brain.

"You're quiet, Ron," I heard Frank say, but I ignored him, too sickened to bother looking in his direction.

Let them throw me in prison, I thought as we landed at Heathrow and rolled down the runway. *I don't bloody well care anymore.*

We got into Frank's car in the airport car park and made our way back to Kingston. The other two talked about how great the holiday was and what fun we had, but I said nothing. I was glad to be on UK soil.

Dudley was dropped off first and Frank stopped the car outside my block of flats. I opened the door and went to climb out. Frank put his hand on my arm.

"I'll pick you up tomorrow," he said.

"No," I said. "You won't." My heart was beating 100 miles an hour.

"But it's Sunday." Frank looked at me with bewilderment. "We always meet on Sundays."

"Enough is enough. I'm not doing this any more," I replied.

"But…"

"I want you to leave me alone." I looked at him with hate.

"I'll tell your parents…"

"Go on then!" I interrupted in a scream, which made Frank jump and reel back. I could feel the fury and the pent up years of bitterness and frustration boiling to the surface. I wanted to punch him in the face. I wanted to batter him till he stopped breathing. "Go on then you pervert! Come in with me and you can tell them now. In fact, I'll tell them for you if you like!" I got out of the car, walked to his side of the vehicle and bent forward to look down at him in the driver's seat. He hadn't closed the window. "Come on then! Out of the car!"

Frank's face was red and his mouth hung open in shock. He began to stutter something but I cut him off.

"Do what you like. Tell the police. Tell my mum and dad. I don't care any more!"

He was on the verge of tears and his chin was trembling. "No, please don't tell anyone," he said in a wobbly voice. "Don't say anything to your parents. Please, Ron. Please, please... I beg you."

In silence I pulled my case from the boot and walked off. I didn't look back as I heard his car drive off. I was shaking from head to foot but I felt fantastic. Calling his bluff had worked. The lift was broken so I climbed the 12 flights of stairs to get to our flat. Tears trickled over my cheeks. But they weren't tears of sorrow. I was free.

11

I explained to my parents that I didn't want to see Frank anymore because he was close to Dudley and I felt left out, what with them being uncle and nephew. They also understood that I was nearing 16 and wanted to spend my spare time with friends of my own age. It was a relief that they didn't ask any awkward questions and that my abuser was out of my life for good. The anxiety that dogged my days since I was nine didn't disappear – nor did the bad memories – but it felt as if the weight of the world had been lifted off my shoulders and there was something I desperately wanted to do. I was a 15 year old boy and I felt that I needed to try and enjoy the rest of my youth.

From the day I got rid of Frank I began to feel just a little of my real self come back to me, bit by bit. It was a slow process and I still didn't confide in anyone but the pressure of keeping up appearances and hiding my pain wasn't there anymore. However, the nightmares never went completely and I was still afraid of the dark.

In the days after I told Frank to leave me alone I was filled with hope and optimism; it was almost like a buzz or a high. I called around for my friends and we spent all weekend kicking a football about in the park. Paul and Loretta commented that I was full of jokes and couldn't stop singing and dancing about like an idiot.

The food parcels ceased immediately and gradually Frank stopped being mentioned by my parents. Dad still had a job as a paint sprayer in a local garage with his brother Syd and Mum was working in a laundry and cleaning offices so although we were far from well off, we weren't destitute. Plus, it was nearly time for me to leave school and I could bring another wage into the household.

Unfortunately, I left without any exams and was faced with a job in a factory. Mum spotted the ad in the local paper and I was mortified when I was offered the role after the interview, where I had slouched in my chair and answered any questions in mumbles. I think they must have been desperate to fill the position. I spent my days layering bags of tobacco and different types of confectionary into boxes and packing them tightly into neat rows. It was mind-numbingly dull and I dreamt away the time, looking forward to my 18th birthday so I could apply to work in a holiday camp.

Bored out of my skull after 11 months, I left the factory and filled in an application form for a job at a Warner's holiday camp on the Isle of Wight. I wasn't quite 18 so I didn't tell my parents and while I was waiting for a reply they badgered me into getting another job, so I ended up working in a local butcher's, having lied through my teeth, telling the manager that I was experienced in the trade. The role was assistant meat cutter and the pay was £20 a week which was a lot of money back then.

"I'm a pro," I said to the manager in the interview. After all, how difficult could it be, chopping up a few chicken legs? On my first day the manager, Mr Jones, stood watching, open-mouthed when I swung a cleaver over my head and as I whacked it down it sliced a joint of lamb in front of me on a large marble slab. But the instrument got stuck in the bone, so I grappled with it and eventually managed to yank it out with both hands. My grip on the handle wasn't tight enough though so the cleaver flew out of my grasp and ricocheted backwards across the room. Luckily Mr Jones ducked just in time otherwise there would have been a serious injury, if not, a death. The cleaver flew about 20 feet and landed in the window display, amongst pork chops and trays of mince. When I turned to look at my boss his face was red with fury. His blue eyes glinted menacingly at me from behind his round glasses.

"I thought you said you had experience!" he boomed.

Mr. Jones wasn't a small man and he had a rather scary look about him. I could tell that he was someone you wouldn't want to mess with.

"I help my mum in the kitchen," I said.

"What?!" he yelled. "This is a professional butcher shop, not Mummy's kitchen! You could've killed me! Now get that apron off and get out!"

I undid the apron and placed it on the counter.

"Go on. Piss off," he said and his thumb jerked towards the exit.

I walked to the door when it hit me that it was nine in the morning. I had started work at 8:30 which meant that I was owed half an hour's pay. I stopped and looked at Mr Jones. His mouth was twisted into a thin line and his fists were clenched at his sides.

"Erm, Mr Jones," I said. "You owe me half an hour's pay... I think it works out to about... erm..." I tried totalling it up on my fingers.

Before I could say anything else he flew towards me. "Get out of my shop now you useless little fucker!"

I did as I was told.

The next day I got a letter from Warner's saying my application was successful and they wanted me to start the following week. I was in the flat alone and jumped up and down and yelped with happiness. I began singing 'Little White Bull' and I danced around the living room. My wish had come true. At last I was going to be a green coat.

When my parents got back that evening I gave them the news and after some tears from Mum they agreed that I could leave home. It was two days before my 18th birthday and they knew that I was desperate to go, so it was clear that nothing would stop me.

"You will come back at the end of the season, won't you love?" sniffed Mum in her hair net.

"I'll be back at the end of the summer," I said. "You don't need to worry about me anymore, Mum."

"He's a big boy now, Win," agreed Dad. "Good luck, son."

"We'll miss you," smiled Mum. "Won't we, Wally?"

"Yep," nodded Dad.

I felt a lump in my throat. My parents meant the world to me. I was going to miss them.

In May 1966 I was just a few days past my 18th birthday when I got off the ferry at Ryde on the Isle of Wight and headed to Warner's holiday camp in St Clair, along with all the other people who were starting at the same time as me. The management had sent a coach to pick us up from the ferry and I had got chatting to a few of the people on the journey with me. Some were working in the kitchen, others were waitresses and there were two or three entertainers, like me. There was a buzz of excitement as we drove down a steep hill, through winding roads, and got our first glimpse of the site, which was set in pretty gardens and was dotted with rows of wooden chalets, where the guests stayed. When we got off the vehicle we were met by the entertainments manager, Don Hughes, a tall skinny man in a green coat uniform who peered at us over wire-rimmed glasses with cracks in the lenses.

He showed us around the ballroom, which had a glitter ball over the dance floor and a stage at one end. We were given a tour of the shop in the reception area, and then the games room which had a snooker table, video games and a dart board, surrounded by basic Formica chairs and tables.

Don took us to look at the tennis courts and swimming pool and I noticed how lovely the gardens were kept, with beds brimming with flowers in pinks and blues. Through a gate at the bottom of the site guests could make their way to the beach which was about a 100km walk. Don told us that when the tide went out you could almost walk to Portsmouth.

We were given our uniforms and taken to our chalets, where we were to live for the foreseeable future. My digs were a small room, lit by a bulb that kept flashing, a metal bed with a biscuit thin mattress and brown and yellow striped curtains at the windows with holes in. But I didn't care. To me it was a palace.

When I got changed from my jeans and tank top into the green coat, white shirt and beige trousers, along with white plimsolls I looked at myself in the mirror on the dresser. I felt very grown up and proud of my new uniform, only I looked more like 15, not 18. I puffed my chest out, trying to fill the jacket which was a size too big for me, but gave up. Mum had always said that I'd grow as I got older but it didn't happen.

Don told me that I was to be sports entertainer, which entailed arranging the day activities for the guests and playing football, cricket and squash with them, so he quickly gave me the nickname 'sporty'. In the evenings I had to add a bowtie to my uniform and mingle with the guests, ensuring that everyone was happy. That was my favourite part of the job and on the first night, when I entered the ballroom, where everyone was gathered for drinks and to watch the entertainment, I immediately noticed how many attractive girls there were.

The glitter ball was throwing light across the walls, the sound system was playing the latest chart hits and I felt a rush of adrenaline hit me as I made my way amongst the crowds. Girls smiled at me and their mothers waved and asked me to join them. Men shook my hand. Everyone wanted to talk to me now I was a member of staff. I felt famous. My green coat was like a brightly shining flame to numerous moths. Over the following weeks I slept with girls on the beach, in their chalets and even in the sports equipment cupboard. I noticed that women weren't interested in the other male guests. It was seen as a coup, bagging a green coat, and the girl could return home and brag to their mates about their conquests. The male staff at Warner's were the prey of the female guests – young, middle-aged, aunts, divorced mothers and married, bored housewives, whose husbands had drunk too much and staggered back to their chalets, leaving their women to go on the rampage.

I was 18 and it was my first taste of freedom. I couldn't walk five metres without a lady stopping me and asking me to pose with her for a photograph. It did my confidence the world of good. I felt like a sex God.

Every evening, for an hour, before the cabaret began, it was my job to be a bingo caller in the ballroom and on my fifth night there I got up on stage with a microphone in hand and began spinning the basket with the numbered balls in and shouting out: "Two fat ladies – 88!" and so forth. I was in my element and after a few minutes I got so carried away that I forgot to shut the trap door on the basket and I gave the handle on the contraption a good shove. All 90 balls flew out of the basket, bounced across the stage and in between the tables where the guests sat. There was uproar when everyone crawled along the floor, grappling around, sending chairs flying, trying to catch the things.

I pointed at a group of women scrabbling about on their knees: "Blimey, watch me balls!" I yelled. "Don't grab 'em too hard! You'll do me a mischief!"

I turned to a woman who had a handful of balls and she was holding them out to me.

"These look like yours, love," she said and dropped them in my hand, grinning.

I winked at her. "Thanks for keeping them nice and warm, love!"

"Anytime. I'm a well practiced ball handler," she said and handed me a piece of paper and walked off. I unfolded it and saw a phone number scribbled in eyeliner. She was a cute blonde so I put the paper in my pocket and went about collecting the rest of my errant balls.

However, as I happened to look towards the front row of chairs in the audience I noticed Don's angry eyes glinting out from behind his broken lenses. He strode over to the stage in the tatty dress suit and shiny shoes he wore in the evenings and ordered the band to start playing.

"Get off stage you clumsy pillock!" he shouted. I did as I was told.

It was nearing the end of the summer season. One Saturday night I was in the ballroom, making sure that the guests were happy, when I noticed a slim brown-haired girl dancing with her friend to Cliff Richard's 'Summer Holiday'. She looked different to many of the other guests because she wasn't smothered in make-up and didn't seem drunk. When she sat down at her table I approached her and asked her if she was having a good time.

"Yes thanks," she said and smiled shyly. I thought she had beautiful eyes.

"I'm Ron," I said and sat next to her. I wasn't usually nervous when it came to talking to the guests, as it was my job, but there was something about this girl that I really liked.

"I'm Margaret and this is my sister Caroline. She works here."

"Hi Caroline," I said. "I thought I'd seen you around."

"I'm the children's auntie," she said.

Both girls lived with their parents on the island and it turned out that Margaret loved coming for a dance with her sister at the holiday camp. I sat and watched the entertainment with them and arranged to meet Margaret the next night.

On my day off we took a coach trip around the island and Margaret showed me the sights. That night she took me back to her home for dinner, to meet her parents, Betty and Ron, who were very welcoming. It was the end of the season and the camp had just closed and they invited me to stay with them, which I did for a week or so. But I missed Mum and Dad and wanted to go back and see them until it was holiday season again. I called them the day before I was due to go home.

"Hi Dad," I said, when he answered the phone.

"Ron! How are you? How's that new lady of yours?"

"Fine, Dad. She's great. I'm coming home tomorrow."

"What?"

"It's the end of the season," I reminded him.

"But we thought you were living with Margaret's parents."

"No, I stayed with them for a few days, after the camp shut. Nothing indefinite."

"Oh."

"What's up, Dad?"

"We didn't think you were coming back, so we moved into a one bedroom flat. It's nicer than the other one. No mice and the lift works."

"But what about me?" I couldn't believe they would move without telling me.

"The last time you rang you said you were staying with Margaret so when the council made the offer we decided to take it. We've been on the list for an exchange for ages."

"OK, Dad. It's not a problem. I'm happy for you."

"Sorry, Ron, seems like it was a misunderstanding. You will come and visit though?"

"Sure, Dad. I'll see you soon."

"OK, Ron."

That phone conversation took place at the end of September 1966. By the Christmas Margaret and I were married.

12

Margaret was a nice, decent girl and I was genuinely fond of her, but we were both 18 and had only been together for three months when we walked down the aisle on 17th December 1966. I hadn't really had the time to think about it all that much because Betty, Margaret's Mum, had suggested that we get engaged as I was now living with them and in those days 'living over the brush' was a cardinal sin. When we said that we would consider getting engaged she then went around the neighbourhood announcing to everyone that we were getting married by Christmas. She was a lovely lady, although a bit pushy and we didn't have the heart to disappoint her. As soon as she spotted the hastily bought £20 gold plated engagement ring on her daughter's finger she was like a ferret down a drainpipe when it came to sorting the nuptials. I have never seen anyone arrange a wedding as quickly as Betty.

I thought I was in love so I wasn't overly bothered and as I had no home in Kingston to go back to I reasoned that the Isle of Wight was a good place to live. Since my first holiday there at 15 I had been fond of the island. I don't think I was all that romantic or practical at 18 and hadn't considered what married life involved.

My parents weren't too impressed and said that I was too young but eventually they agreed it was up to me. Being pretty laid back I just went with the flow and as Betty and Ron had been so kind to me I didn't want to let them down.

Margaret glided down the aisle of St John's church in Ryde in white frills and layers of ruffles and I wore my very first suit and tie. I thought I looked the bees knees. Pauline's husband John was my best man and he winked at me as he handed over the rings during the ceremony. Both sets of parents looked on proudly and after the service we all walked to the parish church hall. It was a cold and rainy day so when we got there we were all soaked through, but no one seemed to care too much and 20 guests sat down to a main meal of roast beef, surrounded by pink and yellow balloons that Betty had blown up herself. John stood and did a speech but being the quiet, shy sort it only lasted about 10 seconds.

The wine and beer were flowing freely so by the time the dessert turned up a few of the lads in Margaret's family were well oiled and one of them flicked a spoonful of jelly and ice-cream across the long trestle table where we were all seated. Soon the whole room erupted into a huge food fight. I stood to tell everyone to calm down and heard a loud yell of "Geronimo!" which was accompanied by a face pack of lime flavoured jelly. It clung onto my chin and coated the front of my suit. With jelly coating my eyelashes I blinked down at my new wife, seated at the side of me, whose brilliant white dress was now mottled with patterns of colourful dessert.

She didn't look happy and sniffed "my lovely dress!" so I picked up my plate and flung it across the room, before ducking under the table, where I was met by my mum and dad, who appeared shocked by the riot. The noise and laughter from above was deafening as jelly ricocheted across the place and splattered on the floor nearby. One of the guests had brought their dog and he was having a whale of a time licking up the sticky mess. Mum looked at me with ice cream nestling amongst the decorative cherries on her new wedding hat. A lump of green jelly wobbled on its wide brim and fell onto the front of her dress.

"I paid a fortune for this sodding hat," she huffed.

Margaret and I rented a tiny cottage up the road from the church in Ryde and moved in a few days after we married. It was furnished with a lumpy old sofa and a few cabinets and had an electric fire in the living room that threw out a pitiful amount of warmth from the one bar that was working. Margaret and I were so cold we huddled under blankets in two jumpers each, as well as gloves, hats and scarves. We couldn't afford a TV so we watched the mice chase each other up and down the room, dashing in and out of holes in the floorboards. At night we could hear them chewing through wires and any food we had in the cupboards. I don't know what we expected married life to be like, but it certainly wasn't this. I had had no job since I left the holiday camp and any savings I had in the bank were nearly gone and Margaret had a part time job in a hardware shop. We couldn't even afford to buy a gas heater or to rent anywhere better and, one night, when rain began to pour through the living room ceiling onto our heads we decided we couldn't take the cold any more, so I called my sister and asked if we could live with her in her and John's three bedroom flat in Kingston, Surrey. Pauline said it was fine. Margaret and I bid farewell to her parents, packed some clothes and were on the next ferry over to the mainland.

Pauline and John were welcoming and gave us their spare room to sleep in but by then they had a three year old daughter, Lynne, and the flat was very small, so I put my wife and I on the council list, hoping that we would be housed soon. Margaret found out she was pregnant a few months after the wedding so it was time to find a job. I was yearning to go back to work in a holiday camp but there weren't any such places in Kingston and although I wasn't happy to be living back in the town where I had escaped bad childhood memories, I was a married man and I had responsibilities. But if ever I had to go into town I always avoided walking anywhere near Frank's grocer's shop. It sometimes crossed my mind that he could be doing the same things to other kids but I am sad to say that I just didn't have the courage to tell anyone. I was so ashamed of my secret.

The nightmares were less frequent, but Margaret had woken me up several times, asking me what on earth was wrong, as I had been yelling out in my sleep. I couldn't tell her or anyone else about the abuse. How would any woman want me if she knew the truth? I hid my secret deep down inside and reminded myself that no one must ever find out. With Margaret at my side, and a child on the way, I was safe. I did my best to live as normal a life as possible.

Margaret and I were in the middle of the supermarket, picking up sausages for dinner when all of a sudden her legs buckled underneath her and she fainted out cold on the floor. She was seven months pregnant, so of course I went into immediate panic mode and screamed out as I darted up and down.

"My wife's fainted!" I dropped to my knees to give her mouth to mouth resuscitation. I took in a big breath and then blew it into her lungs and pumped at her chest.

"Wake up, Margaret!" I bellowed. "Breathe, breathe!"

I repeated the same actions several times, blowing lung-full's of oxygen into her, but she didn't flicker. A small crowd had gathered around me and were making concerned noises and then I felt a hard tap on the shoulder. I stopped what I was doing and looked up. A middle aged woman in thick eye make-up frowned down at me.

"Oi, love. D'you mind me asking what're you doing down there?" she asked.

"Giving my wife mouth to mouth resuscitation, of course," I snapped as my eyes rolled to the heavens. I took another big breath and turned to Margaret to carry on. The woman prodded me on the shoulder again, but more sharply this time.

"Yeah?" I asked, annoyed.

"She's pregnant," The woman pointed to Margaret's large stomach.

"Funny, I hadn't noticed…" I leant down towards my wife again.

"She doesn't need the kiss of life, love," the woman said. "She's fainted. She needs to get to the hospital."

"Oh," I said and stood up.

One of the staff in the shop called an ambulance and Margaret came around during the drive there. We were told that it was nothing unusual for a pregnant woman to faint and that the baby had turned around in the womb for the first time, which had caused her to black out.

Near Margaret's due date we thought we would visit her family on the Isle of Wight, for a bit of a break, but one night she went into labour and this time I managed to stay calm and I phoned an ambulance, which took us to St Mary's hospital on the island. The doctors were worried about the baby's heartbeat so while they performed a Caesarean I was in the waiting room with Margaret's parents, pacing up and down. I was beside myself with worry, but a few hours later our daughter, weighing 6lb 3oz, was born. The first time I held her I felt like sobbing. I stroked her fuzzy blonde hair and stared down at her in my arms.

"A baby," I mumbled to myself and smiled at Margaret, who had just been sewn up after the operation and couldn't hear me because she had fallen into an exhausted sleep.

"Hello, Suzanne," I whispered, gazing at my daughter. I couldn't believe that I had managed to produce something so perfect and beautiful. Betty kissed me on the cheek and said, "Congratulations – Daddy!" I had never felt happier or prouder at hearing myself being called a father. I couldn't hold back the tears.

13

The council gave us a three bedroom house in Wallington, Surrey, but we couldn't afford furniture so a sofa, fridge, wardrobes, a bed and things for the baby were bought on credit. I got a job as a postman, but had to leave after a day because I was badly bitten on the backside by a Yorkshire Terrier. Margaret wasn't impressed that I had lost my job so quickly. We were arguing a lot and it was always about the same subject – money. Fortunately, I landed another job, as a bus conductor. I had a great time, travelling up and down Surrey and the outskirts of London, ringing the bell and chatting to the customers. I even practised my Tommy Steele and Norman Wisdom impressions on them.

In April 1969 we had our second daughter, Lorraine, and I thought I was the luckiest man on the planet. We were broke and had a lot of debts due to buying so much on hire purchase, but I loved being a dad and taking the girls to the park to feed the ducks and reading them stories. I wanted to keep them safe and was wary of strangers being anywhere near them. I only wanted close family around my kids. I reminded Margaret that there were some dangerous people in the world and that we should ensure the girls were safe at all times. I think she just thought I was being protective.

The situation had got so bad financially that Margaret's mother moved in for a while, to help out where she could. Betty and I got on well but it hurt my pride. I was working as many shifts as possible but the money still didn't cover the debts and Margaret and I bickered instead of talking. Looking back on it I think I was a proud and devoted father, but not as good at being a supportive husband. I tried not to worry about it and concentrated on arranging the girls' christening.

The new estate where our house was built wasn't completed and had no church but did have a resident vicar so we spoke to him and he said he would be happy to carry out the service at home. On the day of the ceremony we dressed Suzanne and Lorraine in flowing white robes that we bought on HP and cleaned the house until it was spotless. Both sets of parents came, as well as my sister and John. Everyone was in their finery, waiting for the vicar to turn up. The doorbell went and in he walked, wearing yellow Wellington boots with a big bag under his arm. He stood at the foot of the living room and introduced himself and said a few religious words to kick the service off.

"We haven't got a font, vicar," I interrupted, not knowing how he was going to bless my children.

"Don't worry, Mr Sheppard," the young man smiled and held up his bag. "I've thought of that. We can use this."

He unzipped the bag and dangled a large Pyrex dish in the air, looking pleased with himself.

I saw Margaret and my mother's mouths drop open. The others glanced at each other in amazement.

"That's a Pyrex dish," my dad said, pointing at it with a frown.

"It's perfectly big enough," said the vicar, showing disappointment on his face. "I couldn't find anything else."

I looked at the floor, trying not to laugh. The sight of him looking gormless in his wellies and swinging a cake bowl was too much.

"It's alright, vicar. Do you want some water for it?" asked Margaret, trying to be encouraging, which only made me worse.

"No, but he'd like some eggs and flour," I said.

The vicar nodded; relieved, and asked her to half fill the bowl under the tap, to use as holy water for the blessings and as he read passages from the Bible I was asked to hold Lorraine over the bowl while he dripped water on her head. The baby screamed and her foot knocked the dish, sending splashes of water onto the carpet and the vicar.

"Oops a daisy!" he went and then carried on with his sermon.

I couldn't hold it in any longer and felt my shoulders begin to shake. I caught my dad's eye, who was desperately trying not to laugh as well. I quickly passed the baby to Margaret.

"Sorry," I mumbled. "I need the loo."

I ran to the bathroom and held onto the sink while I sniggered. I then washed my face with cold water, regained control of myself and joined the others in the living room. Afterwards I shook the vicar's hand and thanked him.

"But the next time you might want to bring a washing up bowl instead so we could do the dishes at the same time and get two jobs done at once," I said.

The vicar blushed, but he was a nice young man and didn't take offence.

Soon I lost my job because the buses were running without conductors. Our debts were growing out of control and Margaret and I were arguing morning, noon and night. We were both only 20 years old but I felt 100. I realised that I'd got married too young, but we had two kids and it was too late to regret anything now. I loved my children. We had to get on with it. I scoured the newspaper for jobs but there was nothing. We were desperate; the fridge was empty and we had final demands dropping through the letterbox like junk mail.

"Stop buying stuff from that bloody book!" I yelled at Margaret one evening after we had bathed and put the kids to bed. She had several mail order catalogues and as soon as my back was turned she ordered clothes and toys for the girls. She reasoned that the payments were monthly so we wouldn't notice them, but each item mounted up and she had bought so much that our bill each month was astronomical.

"I'm sick of being broke, Ron! The girls need new shoes!" She cried.

"They can make do with what they have. If we get in any more debt we'll be kicked out of the house! We can hardly pay the rent as it is!"

"Go and find a job then!" she yelled.

"What do you think I've been doing? There isn't anything out there! I've been looking!"

"Look harder then!" Margaret yelled, tears streaming down her face.

"Thanks for your support!" I shouted.

Margaret stormed out, slammed the door and went to the bedroom. I sat in front of the TV on my own for the rest of the evening. There were countless nights like that.

The next day I went to the Army recruitment office to sign up. I hated the idea but they gave each new recruit a day's wage straight away as an incentive. I took the money and was told that in two weeks I would be going to Catterick in Yorkshire for training. I felt as if my life was over. When I told Margaret she wasn't happy about my leaving but I had signed the Queen's allegiance and there was no backing out of it. I was going to be a soldier.

Two weeks later I was on a coach to Catterick Army training camp to join the 2nd Royal Tank Regiment. The other new recruits on the coach chatted but I stared out of the window, feeling sick.

The coach drove towards the Royal Armoured Corp HQ which was an imposing sight - surrounded by a high wire fence that was manned by armed guards. As we made our way past the security check point I spotted numerous huge Army tanks and behind them were several assault courses. I gulped with fright. I wished I'd never joined up.

When we got off the coach we were met by the person in charge of platoon training, Sergeant Major Taylor, who I immediately referred to as Bluto because he looked just like the baddie from 'Popeye' with his muscle-bound frame, wide neck, and he was about 6'4. Once we had been shown the barracks – a sombre-looking room with metal lockers and no carpets - and told to change into our brown Army uniforms we were then ordered to line up on the parade ground. I copied the other men and stood there, straight as a board with my hands at my sides, looking ahead. I was particularly fond of my beret with its red plume but it was too big and kept slipping down, so I had to flick my head back to keep it off my face. I noticed that the other men around me were much taller and beefier than me and I felt self conscious.

Bluto strode outside and stood in front of the group, eyeing us suspiciously. He then slowly walked down each line of men and glared at us one by one. Occasionally I heard him bark in his Geordie accent, "Tie that bootlace!" or "stand up straight, man!"

When he got to me I peered nervously at him from under my beret. I could hardly see.

"Who are you?" he demanded.

"Ron,"

"Sir!" he bellowed.

"Ron, sir," I said.

"Ron who?" he demanded.

"Sheppard."

"Sir!" he yelled.

"Sir," I said.

Bluto was red in the face and I could see the hairs up his nostrils.

"Straighten your beret!" he shouted.

I did as I was told.

"What are you grinning at you scrawny little weasel?" Sneered Bluto. I wasn't aware that I was grinning. It must have been a nervous reaction.

"Nothing," I said.

"Sir!" he screamed until his head shook and the veins on his forehead stuck out.

"Erm... Sir..."

"I'm going to be keeping my eye on you, Sheppard!" he said and made his way to the next recruit.

He was further down the parade and picking on one of the others when I got bored and I took a few steps out of line and began pacing about with my chin jutted forward. I stuck my chest out in a barrel shape like Bluto's and strutted up and down, doing the Hitler salute. The other men in the line next to me began laughing which egged me on.

"Yes sir, no sir, three bags full sir!" I barked while doing an exaggerated frogmarch. The men were now in fits and I was getting carried away; my legs kicking up higher and higher, my arms practically swinging themselves out of their sockets. I was adding the Hitler moustache with my two fingers placed above my top lip when I felt a tap on the back of the head. I stopped what I was doing and looked to my side. Bluto was standing there; fluorescent pink in the face and shaking with rage.

"What the hell do you think you're doing, Sheppard?!" He grabbed me by the front of the shirt and shook me.

"Nothing... sir..."

"You've been here two minutes and already you're trying my patience, you puny little runt! Now get down and give me 50 sit-ups!"

"But I can only do five," I said. I wasn't sure I could manage that many.

Bluto looked like he was about to kill me so I fell to the ground and began wheezing through 50 sit-ups. It took me an hour, by which time he had sent the other men back into the barracks. When I finished I dragged myself to my feet. Bluto grabbed my shirt front again, lifting me off the ground, and I felt his spittle spray my face while he spoke.

"Annoy me once more, runt, and I will make you pay. Get it?"

"Yes," I answered.

"Sir!"

"Sir," I said.

How I got through the six weeks' training I'll never know. The assault course was way beyond my capabilities and I wasn't strong enough to pull myself up the ropes and over the obstacles. The first time I attempted to get over the 15 foot wall on the course I couldn't do it so Bluto asked another recruit to give me a leg up. I had to take a running jump and the other squaddie launched me up in the air with his hands. Instead of landing on top of the wall I flew about 20 feet and landed in a pit of mud and water on the other side. The time I did manage to yank myself up onto the same wall by a rope I got stuck and Bluto had to get two of the other recruits to help me down, earning me the nickname 'daisy' from Bluto. That day the air was blue, he ranted at me so much.

I lost count of the amount of times I was ordered to do the assault course, to run ten laps of the parade ground or carry out night duty as a punishment. One night Bluto ordered me sit in a tank until six o'clock in the morning and then report to him when I'd finished. I'd been caught singing 'Little White Bull' while on parade in front of one of the highest ranking officers in the platoon.

"Now get on with it, Sheppard!" He yelled and left me guarding the tank. It was 10pm. By 11 I was snoring, sprawled out underneath the huge vehicle. I felt a painful kick in the backside.

"Daisy! 100 sit-ups! Now!" Bluto's thick frame blocked the light from the barracks as he loomed above me. Once I'd finished he shouted at me some more and threatened to get me kicked out of the Army. When he stormed off I followed ten paces behind him, mimicking his daft walk and doing the Hitler salute. When he turned and caught me he pushed me in front of him and kicked me in the backside, so I went flying into the entrance of the barracks and landed on my knees.

"I fucking hate you, Sheppard!" Bluto yelled.

I didn't care. I was hoping that I wouldn't make the passing out parade and that I could leave the Army.

The next day we had to march around the grounds, with Bluto in front with his chest puffed out, his arms going like pistons, while he barked "heft, height! Heft, height!" This always made me laugh because he never said "left, right". I was caught mimicking him again and was ordered to do 20 laps of the grounds. It was dark by the time I staggered back to the barracks, where I was ordered to clean the toilets with my toothbrush.

As the end of our training period loomed Bluto took great pleasure in telling me at every opportunity that I was going to be posted to Honor in Germany, where I would be sent on a NATO exercise in minus zero temperatures. So, I began plotting a plan to get out of the Army. I liked my home comforts and sleeping next to a woman, not sharing a room with 30 sweaty, farting men, although I had made a couple of friends. I also hated snow and was not prepared to freeze in sub-zero conditions in Germany for Queen and country.

It was a freezing cold November in 1970 when the day of my passing out parade dawned. Bluto came into the barracks and paced up and down between the bunks, checking our uniforms and our beds. Everyone else got a nod from him and stood at ease. When he stopped in front of my bed he glared down at me.

"What d'you call these, Daisy?" he growled, picking up my boots off the floor and swinging them by their laces.

"Boots, sir."

"I can see what they are, you little prick, but have you polished them?"

I knew what a stickler Bluto was for perfection so I had spent an hour shining them. I could see my face in the leather. "Yes sir," I said.

"Not good enough!" He walked to the window, opened it and threw my boots into the snow. The men were ushered outside and I watched the passing out parade from the barracks. I didn't mind. It was warm in there and I had hidden a bar of chocolate in my locker.

After a stressful two weeks' leave, where Margaret and I argued non-stop over her buying more stuff from the catalogue, I was actually glad to return to the Army, although I knew I would miss the girls dreadfully. They were growing up fast and I was resentful that I wasn't around to enjoy Sundays in the park and to play games with them.

When I arrived in Germany however I detested it and called my sister to ring my regiment and pretend Margaret was ill and that I needed to return to the UK. When I was called into the Corporal's office and told I could go I almost kissed him and ran out of the camp laughing and waving at everyone.

Two weeks later I was ordered to report to Bovington Army camp in Dorset and I was discharged by the commanding officer for "being a disgrace to the British Army". I was hurt by his comment, as I thought it was unwarranted. But I don't think I was cut out to be a soldier.

Being at home wasn't much better though because Margaret hadn't been keeping up with the bills, even though I had been sending all my wages home. Final demands were dropping through the letterbox every day.

Mum and Dad visited and knew our five-year marriage was on the rocks so they took us all to Pontins in Camber Sands in the summer of 1971, thinking the break would give us the opportunity to work on our problems. The girls loved it but all the holiday did was remind me how much I missed being an entertainer. I wanted my old life back and when I heard that they were looking for a blue coat I spoke to Margaret about it. We both agreed that I should take the job. I was a father now, and when I look back, I think I was selfish. I guess my only excuse was that I was young. Margaret and I separated; she stayed in the house in Wallington with the kids and I worked at the holiday camp under the guidance of the Entertainments Manager, Billy Crush. It was fantastic to be back in the limelight again, but when I had a weekend off I often spent it with Margaret and the girls.

My wife and I hadn't actually had the courage to call time on our marriage yet and sometimes we still shared a bed. But as we were spending less and less time together and were both getting on with our own lives Margaret filed for divorce without telling me. A week after it came through she gave birth to our son, Michael. She had never told me that she was pregnant, but I knew he was mine and when I called her she admitted I was the father, however she refused to let me see him. There was also something else I didn't know. She had been seeing a new bloke and she married him a month after giving birth to Michael. I was happy that she had met a man but I was desperate to see my children. Unfortunately, Margaret had other ideas and went to Social Services, telling them that I was a bad father and that I never provided for them properly, which wasn't true. Her new husband backed up her lies and Sutton Social Services bought everything they said. I was beside myself. I didn't even get to see my new son and he was passed off as Margaret's husband's boy. Margaret said that unless I signed the papers agreeing to her husband adopting all three kids that she would make things very difficult for me in court. If it were now I would fight tooth and nail for my children but I was scared and stupid. Margaret had always been a nice, placid person and I was shocked by her change in personality. I signed those papers and regretted my actions every day afterwards. The judge let Margaret's new husband adopt them and take his name. Even my parents were kept away from my kids and it broke their hearts. I found it hard to forgive Margaret for that. I sat in my chalet in my blue coat uniform on my own and cried my eyes out. Yes, I had always wanted to be an entertainer but I hadn't bargained on losing my lovely children. I would have tried harder in the Army if it had meant keeping them. I felt such a failure. It was a year until I was allowed to meet my Michael and see Suzanne and Lorraine again.

My first dance at Warner's Holiday Camp 1966

My Pontins Days

Mum and Dad at Pontins with Ron 1982

RON and WENG – found love and happiness at last

RON AND WENG (on his right) with EXTRAS as his Ex Wives

RON, YOUR TURN TO BUY FISH AND CHIPS!

RON ON TOUR with SIR NORMAN WISDOM

WAN and RON lasted eight months. He did not know about this
wedding until he got back to Thailand. It was too late then.

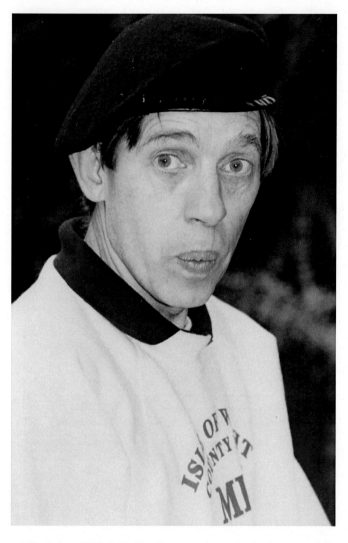

The Isle of Wight MRI Scanner Appeal which Ron initiated
through his Arachnoiditis Campaign – oooh Betty!

Thanks for the support of The Isle of Wight County Press
'The Barron Knights' and Leee John 'Imagination'

First marriage: were we too young though?
But we had three wonderful children.

Face the camera time for a documentary.
'Hidden Lives'

Cabaret Time all over UK as Scott Wilde stage name

My Pontins Blues at Little Canada 1982.
With the young blond Shane Richie as my assistant.
From left to right: Tom, Cathie, Lee, Ronnie, Shane, Me,
Jimmy, Kathy, Lorraine and Jenny my Chief Hostess.

Surprise visit by Simon Ward and Sylvia Syms
at Little Canada collecting for children charity SOS.

Ron meets Roy Barraclough at his first holiday camp.

Shane and I, embracing after a great show at Brean Sands.

Weng and I with the legendary Buddy Greco and his wife Lezlie
At the Encore Awards.

'He told the audience there that I was HIS hero; Buddy has been
married only five times'

14

I stayed at Pontins in Camber Sands for the season and shared a chalet with Mick Miller, who was keen to be a comedian then and later went on to make a name for himself in the business, winning 'New Faces' and appearing on 'The Comedians'. He used the bluecoat job as a springboard to better things, but in the meantime the two of us had an absolute ball that summer. It was 1971 and we were both in our 20's so in between him refereeing the wrestling competitions and me taking bets from the guests on the donkey derby and shoveling up the animals' dung afterwards we went on the rampage. We took girls back to our room, down to the beach, or anywhere else we could find. We weren't all that fussy where we slept with them, to be honest. It was a big campsite, which held 3,000 guests and there were only 15 bluecoats, seven of which were men, so we had our pick of the women. I was on a mission after my marriage break up and was hurt by the way Margaret had ended things between us. There had been a lot of anger and bitterness. The pain I felt from my marriage was still raw but not seeing my children was the worst part. To take my mind off my troubles I buried myself in the bluecoat life and started seeing as many women as possible, who I would often find in the camp's late night cabaret club, which hosted acts like Peter's and Lee and The Beverley Sisters.

It seemed that the ladies couldn't get enough of Mick and me and even though he was thinning on top and I was no champion weight lifter we never went without.

Another one with an eye for the ladies was the DJ Johnny Sinclair, a pretty boy with shoulder length hair and a shirt open almost to his waist which showed off his dark tan. Women would flock to him like pigeons around Trafalgar Square. Every Saturday he and I were on reception duty and it was our task to welcome the new guests and make them feel at home. We kept a look-out for the prettiest girls, giving them a smile and a wink, watching them pass like they were our next prey. And they often were. The male bluecoats knew full well that they had celebrity status and I can't think of one that didn't milk it and sleep with lots of women – unless they were gay. And even the gay men had adoring female fans.

On the last night the manager threw a big end of season party and the staff and guests had a few drinks and a dance. Afterwards all the bluecoats carried on into the early hours, laughing and talking about what a great season we had had. Then it was time to pack our bags and head home.

As soon as I set foot on the coach the gloom descended. I had no wife and kids to return to – and no home. I made my way to my sister's in New Malden, Surrey. She and John had three daughters by this time and the place was cramped with me sleeping on the sofa and living out of a suitcase. After the hedonistic life of the past six months, I had come down to earth with a big bump. But it was time to try and sort something out so I could see my children. Although I had kept myself busy so I wasn't able to focus on them too much, they were always in the back of my mind and I had photographs of Suzanne and Lorraine on my chalet wall. I didn't have any of Michael yet but I hoped that Margaret might send me one. I was desperate to get a glimpse of my son.

I called Margaret and asked if I could see the kids and at first she wasn't keen but then she agreed and brought them around to my sister's house. Of course, Lorraine was younger so she was shy at first and probably didn't realize who I was but Suzanne gave me a big cuddle. It was so wonderful to see them again, even if it was only for a few hours. Margaret didn't bring Michael along and said that her husband wasn't aware that she was there, so she couldn't get him out of the house. I asked her if she could arrange it soon and she said she would try. I didn't want to antagonize her so all I could do was hope. It was such a relief that Margaret and I were on good terms now. We didn't do well together as a married couple but she was a good mother and a decent person.

Margaret also agreed to let my mum and dad see the children too, which was fantastic news. A few weeks later she returned with Tim. It was nearly Christmas and I had bought a pile of presents for all three kids. Michael was the spitting image of me, I thought, and I felt tears well in my eyes as I held him. Margaret and I smiled at one another. The bad atmosphere between us had evaporated and we were able to get along okay after that.

I have always hated bad feelings and try to avoid it. I still often thought of the fear I felt during my childhood and although it wasn't my parents fault that Frank ruined my early years I wanted my kids to have as happy an upbringing as possible. My mum and dad had always done their best for me but they weren't demonstrative people and I often felt alone, particularly when the abuse began. Of course, they didn't know what was going on, but kids want their parents to protect them and the worst part of the situation with Frank was the solitude and helplessness I felt. I wanted to do the best for my children. The guilt I felt at not being able to give them the stability and contentment that comes with two happy parents being together was something I carried for a long time.

I was 23 by then and still a daft kid myself. I thought I was mature but I was far from it. I had a lot of growing up to do and when I look back at myself in those days I can see that I was always running away from reality. And that's exactly why I fell into marriage number two.

In early 1973 I got a job as a bingo caller at the Top Rank bingo hall in Kingston and one night I spotted a pretty blonde girl in the audience. The place was drab and uninspiring and usually filled with middle aged women with big hairdos but the girl wore a lovely fashionable dress in bright red and I couldn't help noticing that she was slim with a fair sized bosom. She smiled at me while I was shouting out the numbers and during my break I walked up to her table to introduce myself.

"What's a lovely girl doing in a place like this – alone?" I asked, hands on hips, in my green nylon suit and dickey bow tie, which was my uniform.

"I love bingo!" she said and I noticed that she had a great smile and a warmth about her.

"I'm Ron. What's your name?"

"Jeanette."

"Pleased to meet you." I held her hand in front of my lips and kissed it.

Jeanette and I chatted for a few minutes and I found out that she was a pregnant 21-year-old single mother and lived in a halfway house for women with her two year old son, Tony. Her boyfriend had left her when he discovered she was expecting and I felt sorry for her. We went out after my shift, for a custard tart and a cup of tea in a late night café, and I saw her once more before she invited me back to her place. While Tony was asleep on his tiny cot Jeanette pulled back the covers on her bed, jumped on it and patted the sheet next to her.

I looked at her, shocked. "What… you mean…?"

She giggled and threw her head back. "Come on, Ronnie, darling…"

Tony was out for the count, so I jumped into bed and we had rampant sex twice.

Pauline was very welcoming and her husband John and the kids were great but I didn't want to keep relying on them so I became a permanent fixture in Jeanette's place. We had to keep quiet though as men weren't allowed in the building and the council might have thrown her out if they knew that I had moved in.

It was a tight squeeze at Jeanette's though, as it was one room with a single bed for her and a tiny one for Tony, a cute little boy with his mother's cheerful temperament and blond locks.

The carpet smelled damp and the wonky wardrobe was crammed with all her belongings. The brown curtains hung off the windows in strips, they were so old. I had lived in some hovels in my time but this took the biscuit.

Jeanette and I were together less than a week when we decided that it would be easier to get a council house if we said that we were a family, especially with the baby being on the way. I needed a home too, so we agreed to get married. And that's what we did – in June 1973. It was a quickly arranged ceremony at Kingston register office and both sets of parents were there. Mum and Dad asked me if I was doing the right thing, but I was adamant about marrying Jeanette. However, I wasn't in love with her and I hadn't given the whole thing much thought. Both of us were lost souls and we were clinging on to one another.

After her son, Paul, was born the council gave us a dilapidated two bedroom cottage in Kingston, which was home to many rats and had no running hot water. I had to fill the bath with kettles of boiling water and the four of us used to have to share it. I felt sorry for the kids, living in such a damp place, and we were constantly wrapping them up in layers of clothing and fretting that they would catch cold. I was still working at the bingo hall but the money was poor and we never seemed to have enough for food and bills. It didn't take me long to realize that Jeanette and I had little in common and that we had come together for the wrong reasons.

When she began leaving me with the boys most nights to go and fritter away any spare cash we did have at the bingo halls in the area I realized that she had a big problem with gambling. I had noticed her love of the game before, after all it was how we met, but now she was using it as an escape from the house and me as a permanent babysitter. The boys weren't mine but they were lovely kids and I was extremely fond of them. Only I was 24 and itching to get back out there and live life to the full again. I felt trapped, gloomy and restless. I spoke to Jeanette and said I was going to take a job at Pontins in Camber Sands again. I was desperate to see Mick and all my old friends. Jeanette simply smiled and shrugged. She didn't say anything or stop me from going. I doubt she loved me either and I expect that she was glad to see the back of me, even though she would never have been rude enough to admit it. It was a shame. She was a nice girl but we were no great romance, and we should have remained friends.

I called Mick and told him I was returning to Pontins. He was happy to have his partner in crime back and I was itching to get on the coach to the camp. Little did I know that I was about to get my heart broken.

15

I returned to Pontins in Camber Sands and it was great to see Mick and all the others but I wanted to branch out a bit, experience-wise, and I found a job at Warner's in Yarmouth, on the Isle of Wight, as the resident photographer. It was my job to spend the days mingling with the guests and taking pictures of them playing crazy golf or in the knobbly knees or ballroom dance competitions. I'd always been interested in photography, ever since my dad gave me a brownie camera, but I really wanted to be an entertainer. It was the April of 1974 and all the performing posts had gone already. Still, it was a pretty place, filled with overflowing flower beds and freshly cut lawns and I was glad to be back on the island. I often thought of my first visit to a holiday camp with my parents when I was 14.

The holidaymakers loved having their photos taken and each morning the manager Jimmy would come and collect the photos from the day before and put them up on the pinboard in reception so the guests could buy them as souvenirs for 50 pence each.

It was my first evening there and I was wearing new shiny black shoes that were tight. I was standing on one foot and rubbing the other against my ankle, it was so sore. The ballroom was filling up with guests and the glitter ball was casting sparkles of light on the walls. I stood gazing at the dance floor which was sunken into the ground and looked very exotic.

Then I felt a tap on the shoulder and heard, "Don't worry, Ron. You'll get used to them." I turned to see an old friend of mine from Warner's called John Emms. He motioned towards my feet and smiled. I couldn't believe it was him and shook his hand, happy to see him. He usually wore leathers and roared around the countryside on a motorbike but he was in a white shirt and black suit. His long hair was slicked with gel and tied back into a ponytail. Today he is one of the regular extras in 'Eastenders' and has been for years.

John then asked what I was up to and when I told him he said that he didn't understand why I was taking photos when he knew I wanted to be an entertainer. Although I was a general bluecoat at Pontins I had joined in with the shows occasionally, doing my Tommy Steele and Frank Spencer impressions. I had also presented some shows or acted as master of ceremonies and my confidence on stage had rocketed. I was itching to get back out there.

"You're wasted, just taking snaps of guests," John said. "I'm the entertainment manager and I need an assistant. My number two hasn't turned up, so you're it!"

"But I have to take the pictures all day," I replied. "I can't do both."

"Take the pictures during the day and then join me in the evenings. It'll be great!" John laughed. He was a fun bloke and was popular with the guests, so I was keen to take the job. It also meant that I would have a wage coming in for each role.

I accepted the role and John told me that I was to start straight away, so I milled around the room, smiling at people and welcoming guests. Cilla Black was blasting out of the speakers and people began to dance.

Just as I was about to welcome a group of guests I stopped dead in my tracks. A girl with long wavy auburn hair and a dimple in her chin caught my eye and she was looking straight back at me. We both smiled. It was if a bolt of electricity had shot through me, corny though it might sound. I had never experienced that love at first sight feeling as I did then. I just had to know who she was, so I made my way over to her table, where we locked eyes again and I was amazed at the blueness of them. She was beautiful and I couldn't open my mouth to speak. I was lost for words.

"Oh, how wonderful, have you come to take our picture?" asked the woman next to the girl, who I assumed was her mother. She then introduced herself as Maureen.

I prized my gaze off her daughter and said, "What? Erm... yes."

The beautiful girl and her family posed around the table and after I took a shot of them they finished introducing themselves. I shook her father's hand, who was a dark haired fella called Harry and had a broad Cockney accent, and the girl's younger sister briefly looked up from her Gameboy and gave me begrudging smile. I then turned to the girl with the huge blue eyes and dimple in her chin. Now I was up close I could see the freckles dotted over her nose and smell her perfume. I must have looked completely gormless. But it was love. I was 100% certain of it this time. Eventually I managed to untangle my tongue.

"Hiya," I said. "Erm... erm... Ron, me. I'm me, what about you? Are you... I mean, your name... if you have one... erm... what's your name?" I went to put a hand on the edge of the table she was seated at and missed, slipping downwards and banged my nose on the glass top. I managed to stand up straight and I smiled again, hoping she didn't think I was an idiot.

The girl's father was smirking at me and I saw him wink at his wife and motion his head in my direction.

The girl smiled and showed shiny white teeth. "Jacquie," she said.

"Sit down. I'll get you a drink," said Harry. "What's your poison?" He pushed his chair back and stood up.

"Erm... I'll have half a lager please."

Harry returned with my drink and Maureen told me that they were from Abbey Wood in London. We carried on chatting and suddenly Maureen piped up, "So, are you married?" I didn't know

147

what to say, as I was still married to Jeanette, although we were going to make the separation legal. We just hadn't got around to seeing a solicitor. I didn't want to put Jacquie off though.

"I'm divorced," I said.

"We've both been married before, haven't we, Harry?" said Maureen. "He's the girls' stepfather."

The conversation carried on, until I had to get changed into my green coat uniform. On my way back to the ballroom I heard a smoochy song playing, so I took a deep breath and made my way over to Jacquie.

"Would you like to dance?" I held my hand out towards her, which she took and we sauntered to the dancefloor. I couldn't believe that I actually had this beautiful girl in my arms and when she laid her head on my shoulder I grinned from ear to ear. To me it was a sign that she liked me. At the end of the dance she pecked me on the cheek and we returned to her table. We enjoyed two more dances and when the evening ended I quickly kissed her on the cheek. I had to be discreet as I was in my uniform and we weren't allowed to mess about with guests, not that that had stopped me before. We said goodnight and I wandered back to my chalet at midnight, gazing up at the stars and thinking of Jacquie. As I lay in bed I relived each dance and everything we had said to one another. My stomach was filled with butterflies and I longed to hold her again. It was a wonderful, but unfamiliar feeling. I eventually fell asleep at 5am.

There was no sign of Jacquie on the camp the next day and I walked around taking photos of the guests feeling flat and despondent. Late in the afternoon I was stooping down to take a shot of two kids in a pushchair for their mother when I felt a tap on the shoulder and heard: "Fancy a coffee?" I was so happy to hear her voice and off we went to the nearby café. Jacquie looked even more beautiful than the night before, in her summery clothes and a band holding her thick hair off her face.

We picked a table at the window and on the way back from the counter my hands shook so much that the coffee cups rattled on the tray.

Get a grip, I said to myself. A girl had never had this effect on me before and I was taken aback by the strength of my feelings and reactions. We chatted for an hour or so and then I asked her if she would like to go somewhere the next day as I wasn't working. She said she would love to but would have to ask her parents. She had just turned 18 and I was eight years older, after all. They agreed so I spent another sleepless night in my chalet, impatient for the morning to come, hoping that this would be more than just a holiday romance.

The next day we headed to Sandown and stripped off to our bathing suits, swimming in the sea and flicking water at one another. When we sunbathed I managed to get a look at Jacquie in her purple bikini and noticed what a lovely little figure she had. She was a petite girl of about 5' 2 and to me she was perfect in every way. When we began mucking about and pushing each other on the sand and then had our first proper kiss on a pedalo it took a lot of self control for me to behave myself, but I was a gentleman. I didn't want to scare her off.

"I've had a lovely day, Ron," Jacquie said in her soft London accent while we waited for a bus to take us back to the camp.

"Me too. Can I see you again?"

"I'd like that." She smiled and I felt a stab of sadness that the day had ended.

That evening I sat with her and her parents in the ballroom again and held hands with Jacquie under the table. I asked if they would mind if we took a walk along Yarmouth Castle which was set around the ruins of an old castle by the sea and only a 10 minute walk away from the camp. Her parents agreed and Jacquie and I spent the evening holding hands and walking down the beach, chatting about football, music and our home lives. She told me that she had just come out of a three-year relationship, which she had finished because of his possessiveness and she said that she had hoped that she would meet someone.

Soon it was midnight and I offered to take Jacquie back to the ballroom.

She squeezed my hand. "No, Ron. I don't want to go back yet. I'm thirsty though. Can we go to your chalet?"

"Sure," I said and turned in the direction of the camp. We walked for a few hundred metres down a sandy path that was encased by trees when Jacqui got a stone stuck in her shoe so she stooped down to get it out. There was no one around so we sat down for a moment and before we knew it we were kissing passionately and rolling around on the ground. We were pulling at one another's clothes and eventually made love, under the moonlight, covered in sand. I thought it was the most romantic thing ever. We dressed and wandered back to the camp, where we found her parents leaving the ballroom.

"Had a nice time, you two?" asked Maureen.

I felt my face flush at the memory of having sex with her daughter.

"We had a lovely evening, didn't we, Ron?" said Jacquie and squeezed my hand.

"Yes… yeah… quite lovely, it was," I said. Then we all returned to our chalets after saying goodnight.

Jacquie and her family were only booked into the holiday camp for a week and soon it was time for them to go home. I was gutted and watched as they drove off in their old Ford Estate.

Four hours later I was called into reception because there was a phone call for me. It was Jacquie and she said that she missed me already. It was just what I wanted to hear. This was not a holiday romance after all.

Jacquie had no job at the time so I told her to come back and I would find her work at the camp and she could be with me. Her Mum then took the phone off her and was laughing about the situation but said that we were rushing things and should take our time. My mind was reeling with ideas and plans but we agreed to go away speak the next day. The following Saturday I got on the train to London to meet Jacquie. She was coming to stay at the holiday camp with me and I didn't want her travelling on her own.

She shared my chalet and was my assistant when I took photographs, but soon I had to pack that job in as it was hard being entertainment assistant as well and I was acting as compere between the visiting cabaret acts that began at 11pm. One of the favourites was a bloke called Kenny Baker, who was in 'Star Wars', but he had been a musical cabaret artist for a long time and after songs he'd keep the audience enthralled with a few self deprecating jokes about himself, being a midget.

"Good evening ladies and gentleman!" I ran on stage and smiled before Kenny made his entrance. "Let me introduce to you the man who plays R2D2 in 'Star Wars'… a man who, when on tip toes stands at a staggering three feet tall! His name is Kenny Baker and he's taken a night off from his job as a bouncer for Mothercare to come and entertain us! Put your hands together for Kenny Baker!"

I still had my other green coat duties and was part of the stage show too. Jacquie sat in the audience while I sang Bobby Vee's 'Take Good Care of my Baby'. As the audience clapped and cheered she came running up to me when I came off stage and wrapped her arms around my neck.

"You have such a beautiful voice!"

"Thanks," I said. "One day I'll sing something just for you."

"Oh, I'd like that, Ron," she replied.

Unfortunately there were no actual vacancies at the camp so Jacquie said that she would have to return home at the weekend which meant that we had three days left to enjoy ourselves. I even considered asking her to marry me and although I had discussed the divorce with Jeanette by now and we had moved things along with a solicitor I wasn't sure if it were wise to rush the situation this time. But I still wanted to tell Jacquie how much I loved her and I suggested that we went for a walk to the castle again. It was another beautiful moonlit night and we strolled hand in hand.

"I love you, Jacquie," I eventually blurted and held my breath, praying I hadn't messed things up.

"I love you too," she said.

I grabbed Jacquie and kissed her over and over until the rain began to fall and we were soon soaked.

"C'mon, let's run back!" I yelled. So we sprinted as fast as we could back to the camp. When we got home we stripped our clothes off and jumped in the shower, where we made love and said "I love you" again.

It was soon time to take Jacquie back to London and on the train we discussed getting engaged. We both thought it may be a bit early but we were keen to go ahead in the near future.

On the return journey back to the Isle of Wight I didn't stop grinning. The most beautiful girl in the world loved me. It was an amazing feeling and for the first time in years I suffered sleepless nights out of happiness, not fear.

After two weeks apart we realized that we couldn't be without one another so I packed in my job at Warner's and went to live with my sister in New Malden so I could be near Jacquie and go and visit her at weekends. Several times she came to stay with me at Pauline's and my sister was glad to see me so happy.

"Blimey, Ron," she said one day. "I've never seen you so smitten before! Have you John?"

"No, I can't say I have," replied her husband.

It was my turn to travel to Abbey Wood where Jacquie lived and when I got there Maureen answered the door. She had a strange look on her face and invited me into the living room. A dark haired bloke with a macho look about him sat in an armchair and stared at me when I entered the room. As soon as I saw him I knew who it was and nerves began gnawing at my stomach.

"Hi, Ron," said Jacquie casually. "This is Alan, my ex boyfriend."

We both nodded at one another and Maureen told me to sit next to her on the sofa. She asked me if I'd like a cup of tea and I nodded, unable to speak. Jacquie was sitting in a chair to the side of Alan and was leaning on its arm and speaking to him about everything he had been doing since they parted. They were like old friends, catching up and laughing and joking. I sat there, sipping my tea in silence. Jacquie didn't say one word to me or include me in the conversation. She hardly noticed I was there. I saw Margaret throw me a sympathetic smile or two. I felt humiliated and hurt. It was obvious that Jacquie still had feelings for her ex and that what she had had with me was a rebound thing. All I wanted to do was get out of there. I said goodbye to Jacquie and her mother and got on the train back to New Malden. I cried like a baby in the carriage. Whether anyone saw me or not I didn't care. The pain was excruciating and I had never felt anything like it. A few days later Maureen called me.

"Ron, I thought you deserved to know that Jacquie got back with her ex-boyfriend. I'm sorry," she said.

I had known this was coming but I thought that Jacquie might ring me herself and explain. Still, it was like being punched in the belly to actually hear the news.

"Thanks for telling me, Maureen," I mumbled.

"So sorry, love," she said.

Not as sorry as I was. I had lost the girl I adored, I had given up my job for her and now I was back, living with my sister. But most of all the hurt I felt over Jacquie was the worst. I could get another job after all. I really was fond of Jacquie and it killed me to realize that she had probably never felt the same way about me. Not long after I found out that she married Alan and was pregnant.

16

Soon I got a job at Top Rank bingo hall in Peckham, calling out the numbers. On the first night a big group of women came in and were soon knocking back pints of lager and being rowdy. When I walked on stage this fat lady with acres of blue eyeshadow hollered to her mates: "Fucking 'ell, look at 'im! I've seen more meat on a toothpick!"

I groaned inwardly, hearing my school nickname.

"Show us yer balls then, love!" yelled a woman with earrings like dustbin lids.

I spoke into the microphone: "I haven't heard that one before!"

"I bet his balls haven't even dropped yet!" laughed a woman with boobs oozing over her top.

"I don't mind. I like 'em young!" said someone else.

"I'd 'ave a bit of him, too!" An obese woman chimed in.

"Blimey, Sonia, if you sat on him you'd squash the poor bleeder! I'll look after you, son!" squawked one of the posse.

"Come on, ladies!" I laughed. "There's plenty of me to go around. Now let's get those balls a jigglin'!"

The women clapped and cheered and I began calling the numbers out. In between each one I was met with a rude quip or a loud complaint if they didn't hear the number correctly because they were so busy larking about.

"He's coming home with me tonight!" yelled one of the gang while pointing at me. "I don't care if he is scrawny; I'll shag him! Better than being an ugly fat old bastard like me old man!"

The others howled with laughter and carried on taking it in turns to poke fun out of their men at home.

"My Bernard's cock is so tiny the last time he got it out I got eye strain trying to see it!"

"Well, it's been so long since I had sex with my fella me fanny's healed over!"

I found Londoner's to be friendly but, in general, a scary lot; however I had some fun there.

One night I accepted a lift home off of one of the clientele and on the drive to New Malden she stopped the car in a lay-by and jumped on me. She was an attractive, well spoken woman in her 30s and it seemed impolite to knock her back, so I had sex with her on the back seat of her Volvo. It didn't have very stable suspension so it rocked up and down and made a funny creaking noise while we were at it.

"That was lovely," she said afterwards as we both pulled our clothes on.

I didn't know what to say. "Erm, thanks."

"What's your name?" she asked, doing up the buttons on her blouse.

"Ron."

"Vanessa." She held out her hand for me to shake, which I did. "Pleased to meet you."

"You too," I said and yanked up my y-fronts. Vanessa drove me back to my sister's house and asked if she could see me again. I was still smarting over Jacquie's rejection but I wasn't going to turn a fling down.

"Sure," I said.

"There's something I need to tell you though."

"What?"

"It's nothing too bad – just a small detail I should tell you about before we see each other again," she explained.

"You didn't used to be a man, did you?" I laughed. She looked at me seriously. My stomach did a flip. "Oh God, it's not that is it?"

"Don't be daft!" Vanessa giggled and put her hand on my knee. "Do I look like a man?"

"Not really but you can never be sure."

"It's about my husband…"

"Your husband…?" I said. "You didn't say you were married."

"He's away."

"Oh, I see…"

"He's in Pentonville."

My mouth fell open. "He's in the nick!"

"He won't be out for a while," she said.

"How long?" I looked longingly towards Pauline's front door, shifting in my seat.

"A month."

"A month!" I jabbered. "What's he in for?"

Vanessa looked sheepish and mumbled, "Murder."

"What?!" I shrieked.

"It *was* in self defence…"

I opened the car door, jumped out and ran to Pauline's house like my backside had just caught alight. I never saw Vanessa again. The next day I handed in my resignation. Someone at the bingo hall told me her husband was "built like a brick shithouse". If he found out about me I didn't want to be a sitting duck.

I was very busy arranging a football match for a local girl at that time, so my worries about Vanessa's hubby were soon forgotten. I'd seen Tara's story in the local newspaper and I began sobbing when I read about her plight. She was just five years old and had been born with a hole in her heart. The article said that if her parents didn't quickly raise the £10,000 needed for an operation she was going to die. So, I got my mates together, who were happy to play a charity match, but we realized early on that we needed a celebrity to bring in as much publicity as possible. I approached Tommy Steele and he agreed. I couldn't believe my luck. I was going to meet my hero.

The day of the game arrived and when I first met Tommy I was speechless, but I soon realized what a down to earth guy he was and my nerves went. It was a Sunday morning and the ground in south London was packed with people paying the £2.00 entrance fee and buying raffle tickets. TV news and the local press had been running reports about Tara and people flocked to help. We had so many gifts donated for the raffle that it took nearly an hour to do the draw during half time. Tommy drew the tickets, but he didn't mind as it gave him a rest from running around the field, playing football, which he was brilliant at, being a fit man. The day was a great success thanks to Tommy and the people who came to support it. We made about £700 which went a little way to help raise the money needed for Tara. Luckily, many others made donations from all over the UK and Tara flew to the US for her operation which was a success.

When I told Pauline why I'd handed my notice in at the bingo hall she sighed and said that I should leave the women alone and concentrate on my work. I thought it was fair advice. It was time to find a job and stick at it. Luckily, I didn't have to wait for long because I got a call from Top Rank, asking me if I wanted to train to be an assistant manager in Chester. I was flattered and thought that my Frank Spencer impressions must have caught the eye of one of the bosses of the place. I saw the opportunity as a chance to learn more about the leisure industry and to get up on stage at the same time.

It was June 1976 and although I was hankering to go back to the holiday camps, I told myself that being a bingo caller, as well as a manager, couldn't be so bad. So, off I went to Chester. On the train up there I remembered what Pauline and my mum and dad said about getting on with the job and not messing about with girls. I was determined to knuckle down and keep a distance from the opposite sex. However, it was easier said than done.

Lesley had a sexy Scottish accent and short jet black hair. She worked for Top Rank too and as soon as I set foot in the hotel where the training sessions were taking place I spotted her. At the end of the training days the group would go for drinks at the bar. The others discussed what they had learnt that day, but it didn't take me long to lose interest and I was far more enthusiastic about getting to know the pretty Scottish girl.

The hotel bar was busy on the first night after our arrival. It was full of business types chatting over glasses of wine while music tinkled away in the background. My small group found a table in the corner and Colin, a young guy with an impressive crop of spots, went off to buy the first round, along with one of the others. I took the seat next to the dark haired girl.

"Good here, innit?" I said. "Smashing place."

She looked at me shyly. "Yes, it's very nice."

"How are you enjoying it – the training and all that…?"

"It's OK. You?" she asked.

"It's OK," I shrugged. After a slightly awkward start, we introduced ourselves properly and the conversation warmed up. Within a few days Lesley was my girlfriend.

Maths was never my best subject at school and most of the training during the day was now focused on balancing company books. I hated it. The nights, reading out bingo numbers, were better, but I was getting bored. So I decided to spice things up in the Chester bingo hall by announcing the numbers as Frank Spencer: "Mmm, Betty, it's all the two's – mmm, number 22, mmm!"

The audience laughed and clapped which spurred me on to try out my other voices on them. That evening several women came up to me afterwards and said how funny I was and that they were looking forward to coming to see me in action again. But as I was about to leave for the night I felt a presence behind me. The boss, Burt, a scrawny bloke with a ginger comb-over, was standing there and his expression was far from happy. I could see his watery eyes bulging behind his thick specs.

"My office, Ron," he barked.

"What's wrong?" I asked.

Burt ignored me and marched to his small office at the back of the large hall while I trailed behind him wondering if he'd found out I'd been mimicking him to the rest of the staff. His office always smelt of old socks and coffee.

"Take a seat," Burt said. So I did. "What's your job here, Ron?"

"Bingo caller."

"And what does that involve?"

I looked at him, confused. "Calling bingo numbers..."

"Exactly. It doesn't mean that you can sod about..."

"But…"

Burt leaned forward in his seat. "…or that you can prance about like a tit, putting on silly voices."

"But the customers loved it," I answered, deeply offended.

"I don't care. This is a serious business, not a holiday camp. You're here to do a job, so get on with it."

"I'm an entertainer, Burt…" I tried to explain.

"Mr. Baxter to you. I don't want to have to warn you again, Ron. It's getting late. You can piss off now."

I was fuming as I walked to the bus stop. All I had done was try and entertain the customers. I hadn't committed a crime.

The next night the place was full but I did as I was told and stuck to calling the numbers in my usual voice.

"Do your Frank Spencer!" shouted a woman.

"Yeah, go on!" the lady next to her joined in.

I ignored them and carried on as normal. Afterwards I explained to the woman and her mate that I wasn't allowed to do impressions any more. The woman, a stocky lady with a head that appeared to balance on her shoulders without the help of a neck, snorted.

"I've never heard anything so stupid! Get the manager!" she demanded. Eventually Burt was brought out by one of the other staff and he approached the woman and her friend. Burt's gaunt face twitched with nerves as he spoke to the customers.

"How can I help you?"

"I have an official complaint," said the neckless woman. "We like Ron's impressions and want him to carry on." Her friend murmured her agreement.

"It's company policy to stick to the rules at all times," said Burt. "Ron is the bingo caller so it's his job to stick to calling out the numbers."

"But it's more interesting the way he does it," said the woman, her beefy forearms now folded high above her breasts.

"I'm sorry but it's the rules," repeated Burt. The conversation went on and I stood in the background, thinking what a twerp my boss was. I wasn't keen on the job anyway and thought that if I couldn't enjoy myself then it wasn't worth doing.

Burt again reminded the two women that it was my role to read out the numbers on the bingo balls and nothing else.

"Well I think it's just petty management bollocks, all this," concluded the no-necked woman as she gave up and stomped off. "Never heard such fucking tripe…"

I couldn't have agreed more. The next day I resigned.

I had never been much good at saying "no". I'm still not, although I am a bit better at it. But back then I disliked disappointing anyone. I was staying with Lesley and her parents, having nowhere to live and being out of work, and as they didn't approve of us "living in sin" I agreed when they suggested we get married. The church ceremony was booked for September which was six weeks away. I wasn't so sure that I wanted to get spliced again; however Lesley's mum was excited about the whole thing and her dad Bill was a big brash Glaswegian fella. As I was sleeping on his sofa I didn't have the guts to go against his wishes. They were strict with Lesley and wouldn't have approved of us having sex out of wedlock.

Bill was an Elvis fanatic so he wore a lot of leather, his black hair was greased into a quiff and he had an imposing air about him. The first time I clapped eyes on him I thought he wasn't the type I would want to cross. Neither did I have the courage to tell him that I had been married before and Lesley didn't want him knowing either, so as we quietly waited for my divorce from Jeanette to come through, Lesley's mother talked about the upcoming wedding with great enthusiasm. Bill, her dad, I think, liked me.

"If yous mess ma girl aboot, me lad. You will answer to me. He glared at me as he called me into the hallway of his home one day while Lesley and her mum sipped tea in the living room. "Hear me?"

I gulped and nodded. "Yes, I hear you, Bill"

Bill's eyes went all narrow. "Mr. Watson!"

"Mr. Watson," I repeated.

"As long as we's understand each ootha. Remembering there was something else that he and Lesley weren't aware of. I was petrified it would come out somehow. While Lesley knew about Jeanette, I hadn't told her about my first wife, Margaret. She thought she was going to be wife number two, not three. Although I had intended to admit the truth before we got married somehow I never plucked up the courage. I was worried it might put her off me. So, not only was I wary of her dad, every time we went to visit my parents I was also a nervous wreck.

There one Sunday in particular when my mum almost landed me in it. Luckily she had removed the wedding photo of

Margaret and me which used to be in a frame on the sideboard, but she still managed to slip up. In mid conversation she suddenly asked me how Margaret was. Dad and I glanced at one another and the room fell silent.

"Margaret?" asked Lesley, eyeing me. "Who's Margaret?"

"Did I say Margaret?" laughed Mum. I frowned at her and shook my head.

"Margaret is my friend's wife. Isn't she, Mum?" I gabbled.

"Oh yes," agreed Mum, looking down at the flowery carpet.

I carried on. "She's my friend's ex wife actually. He left her ages ago though. I've not seen her for donkey's years."

Dad stood there, leaning against the living room wall with a cup of tea in his hand trying not to laugh. But my poor mother often got my girlfriends and wives mixed up. It couldn't have been easy keeping up with my love life.

The wedding day was getting closer and still my divorce from Jeanette hadn't come through. Lesley was in a terrible panic.

"Oh my God, Ron!" she cried. "You're going to be a bigamist! The police will turn up at the church to arrest you! I'll be married to a criminal! What will Dad say?"

"Calm down, Les. I'll sort it out," I promised. "We don't need to say anything to your dad though."

"He's paid for the dress and the food and everything. He'll go mad!" Lesley was pacing up and down her parents' living room, biting her nails while tears filled her eyes.

"He won't just go mad, Les. He'll just punch my flippin' head in," I pointed out helpfully.

"Oh God! Oh God!" she howled and slumped on the sofa.

I sat down and put my arm around her. "It'll be fine."

"Will it?" she asked, sniffing. "Do you really think so?"

"Yep." I didn't like to see Lesley so upset. She was a nice girl and I felt it was my fault that everything was going wrong, so the least I could do was try to make her feel better. However, I'm not sure if I believed my own words.

It turned out that there was a big problem with the divorce and as the wedding day got even closer I discovered that my solicitor had forgotten to get Jeanette to sign some paperwork. So when I went to court the judge announced that it would take another six weeks to get everything finalized. I nearly had a heart attack, knowing that Lesley's dad was going to strangle me with his bare hands when we had to tell him what had happened and admit that I was still married. I begged my solicitor and the judge to sort the mess out, reminding them that I was supposed to walk down the aisle in a fortnight. Lesley was a mess too but she'd have been in a far worse state if I had let on that I was about to do a runner. If the judge hadn't taken my side and angrily ordered my solicitor to pay my costs and if he hadn't hurried the process along so I was granted a decree absolute days before the ceremony I think I might well have been on a flight to Torremolinos rather than face Lesley's father. I'd heard that they were always on the look out for bingo callers in the hotels there.

I'd known Lesley less than six months and I didn't love her enough to marry her. I hardly knew her really. But I was trapped into it simply because I didn't have the guts to say "no". So, once again, I was about to become a groom. Being Scottish, Lesley's parents wanted me to wear a kilt but I bravely put my foot down with Fred and in a newly bought beige suit. Lesley and I said our vows at the Wesley Methodist Church in Chester. She looked a picture, smiling widely in a flouncy white dress, with her father walking her down the aisle in his sporran. There were so many guests in the church and at the pub reception that I imagined her parents had invited the whole of Scotland. John, my brother-in-law, was my best man once more.

"I'm not sure I fancy doing this again, Ron," John warned me quietly after the ceremony was over and the guests were milling about outside the church.

"This'll be the last time, John," I nodded. "I don't want any more wives, thank you."

John looked smart in his black suit and tie, but he wasn't keen on getting dressed up and having people gawping at him. Before the ceremony I reminded him for the fifth time not to mention my past wives in his speech and I could tell he was worried about saying the wrong thing.

"I'll hold you to that," he said with a sad sigh. "Any more weddings and I'm going to have a nervous breakdown."

Lesley and I arranged a mortgage on a red brick house in Broughton Clwyd, just across the Welsh border, which we secured with the help of the Greater London Council, through a first time buyer's scheme. It had two bedrooms and looked out over fields and though it was pokey and we didn't have much furniture to fill it, I was proud that we had managed to buy a house. Paying the mortgage on a regular basis was another challenge for me altogether though and my past inefficiencies with money came back to haunt me. I was hardly mature enough back then to run my own life, let alone get involved in another marriage before I'd hit 30 and have the responsibility of a 22 year old wife.

Bill got me a job in a factory, pressing small shields into gas bottles, which I hated with a passion. It didn't take long for the honeymoon period to end and the rot to set in.

Lesley and I were struggling to cover the bills and I was miserable in Wales, traipsing to work past fields smelling of cowpats early every morning, feeling depressed and bored. The arguments began even before we had our first son Lee, a year after we married. While Lesley relished being a mother, she was distant or snappy with me, no doubt exasperated with my inability to take to married life and be a proper provider. I just wanted to escape. I was still hankering after the life in the holiday camps.

One role I did love though was being a dad and just watching my son sleeping in his cot was enough to spur me on. I told myself that I had to work hard in the factory and that I was to forget about my career ambitions. I'd made my bed so I had to lie in it.

I did see my daughters now and again but Margaret's husband still didn't know I had seen Michael once and she wasn't prepared to let me near him again. I wasn't going to lose another child so I had to keep my marriage to Lesley afloat. It meant that somehow I had to get us out of debt and ensure that Lee had the life he deserved.

However, in early 1978 an event took place that was to change everything. I was at work, lifting a small skip of scrap metal with a handle on the side when the handle broke, causing the skip to topple to one side. I felt a terrific pain in my back and I collapsed on the floor.

"Help!" I shouted to my workmate, who came running over.

"What's wrong?" Samuel stooped down and asked, fear showing on his face.

"I can't move!" I cried as waves of agony sliced through my body.

I was rushed to Chester Royal Infirmary in an ambulance. My family's future was looking bleaker than ever.

17

After several tests, including a myelogram, where dye is injected into the spine and then x-rays are taken, the doctor diagnosed me with having a slipped disc and said I would have to go on traction. A fortnight later my back was no better so the consultant announced that the next step was to put me in plaster from my neck to my waist for six weeks. I was then sent home. Lesley had to wash, feed and change me and what with Lee to look after she was worn out. It didn't help our already shaky relationship, especially as I had been off work for several months and we were on benefits. We couldn't pay our bills and were desperately worried, knowing that I wouldn't be well enough to return to my job for at least six months.

"What the hell are we going to do?" Lesley yelled one afternoon while Lee was having a sleep. "I'm going to have to ask my dad for help!"

"No, don't go to Bill. He'll kill me. He already thinks I'm useless."

"Well he'd have the right bloody idea then, wouldn't he?" Lesley shouted. She was preparing potatoes over the kitchen sink and angrily waving the peeler in the air.

"It's not my fault I've got a bad back!" I retorted.

"You're a liability, Ron! That's what you are! What are we going to do till you're back at work?"

"I don't know, Les. I just don't know."

"Well think of something then!" she yelled. "Before we're thrown out on the streets!"

The pain shooting down my legs was unbearable by now and I was returned to hospital where it was decided that I needed surgery. In May 1978, two days before my 30th birthday, I had the operation, only the pain following it was much worse, what with all the stitches in my back and the nursing staff having to turn me over every two hours. In the end I was so pie-eyed on the morphine they gave me I didn't care any about anything any more. I was out of it.

Finally I was allowed home, but it wasn't long before the house was repossessed because we couldn't pay the mortgage. Lesley was seven months pregnant and cried her eyes out when we had to pack our stuff and move to a shabby-looking council place nearby.

"I'm scared, Ron." She looked at me with tears running down her face as she leant her weight on her case to close the lid. She was surrounded by bin bags which held our few possessions. I felt so guilty. It was my job to look after my family.

By the time Lesley gave birth to our second son, Craig, we were really struggling for money and the arguments got worse. Although I was still in constant pain from my back injury and it wasn't long after my operation, I couldn't sit around any longer as we were in real trouble.

Some friends of ours had a band and they needed a lead singer, so I joined them and we performed in the clubs all over the Northwest of England as a comedy/musical act called Wishful Thinking, with me doing impressions of Rod Stewart, Prince Charles and Norman Wisdom. We recorded an album and sold it at venues to bring in extra income and I used the stage name Scott Wilde. Although I was still in a lot of discomfort from my injury, I really enjoyed being in front of an audience again, making people laugh.

Unfortunately my back couldn't take being on the road all the time, so the band broke up after six months which was obviously bad news for Lesley, who showed her displeasure by reminding me I was a moron. Again, I was on the look out for work when something interesting came my way - a temporary job at a local club in Chester, working as a compere with TV entertainers like Vince Earl, who appeared in the 'Comedians' and a major soap on Channel 4. Another act there was Bob Carolgees and Spit the Dog from the kids' show 'Tizwaz.' But my nomadic professional life soon took me elsewhere when the job ended.

Next I was offered the role of entertainments manager at The Holiday Centre in Dawlish, Devon, which came with a house for the summer season. The money was terrible and things were worse between Lesley and me as we could hardly afford food for the four of us. Every time we argued she would swear and call me rude names, which was understandable really. I was trying my best, but it was just not good enough. We owed The Holiday Centre money and we were getting deeper into debt, so, one night, we decided to cut our losses and run. When we told Lesley's parents what a mess we were in I thought back to Bill's warning before we were married. As he drove down to Devon to collect us my stomach was in knots, imagining him being really angry when he got there. Fortunately he simply threw me a withering look and mumbled something about me being a "waste of skin", but it was hard to understand his accent so I couldn't be sure.

He helped us pack the kids and our belongings in his car and took us back to stay with him and Lesley's mum in Chester for a short while, until we were housed by the council again. I had no work and zero income, except unemployment benefit. The arguments escalated. I feared for the boys' emotional wellbeing. Something had to give.

We always met Lesley's family in the pub every Monday, it was dart's night, although I could not play that good, I was invited to join the team, after a few drinks though I could not even see the board, let alone hit it.

We had bailiffs calling around every week asking for money we didn't have, so in the end I had no option but to declare myself bankrupt. I had received £2,000 compensation for my back injury, but we didn't even see the cheque because it went straight to my creditors.

It all became too much for me and I could feel the depression descending. My nightmares about Frank had never disappeared entirely and keeping my secret from Lesley and my family was always an extra pressure on top of the dramas happening in my life. When I was stressed my nightmares grew and I felt anxious again, like I did when I was a child, huddled under my duvet with Scruff, dreading every Sunday as it drew nearer. Or hiding down at the duck pond, wishing I had the guts to jump in and end it all.

I had to leave before I had a breakdown. Lesley really was a good wife and mother during the five years we were together. It was me who couldn't cope with life and it made me ashamed that I dragged people down with me. I felt I had to leave Lesley. So one morning I got up, packed my clothes in a suitcase, said goodbye to my family, and got on a coach to London.

Lesley informed me by phone that her dad was not happy with me and I was warned to stay away from Chester. Our marriage break up was the best thing for Lesley and the boys. They didn't have to listen to our constant rows and soon after I went she met someone else who made her happy. They had a son together. I was pleased for my ex wife but I wasn't happy that history was repeating itself. I was very sad to hear that Lesley had died in 2005, Lesley was a drinker, I was not. Her parents blame me for her death, although I am so sorry for her passing. I am not to blame.

As with my daughters and son from my first marriage, a new stepfather on the scene meant that I wasn't so welcome and eventually, after a few visits here and there, I lost touch with Lee and Craig. Lesley said that her new husband wanted to bond with them properly and she didn't want me ruining things. I tried hard to persuade her otherwise but she was adamant. For weeks I moped around feeling sorry for myself, until eventually I had to make do with the hope that things would settle down, that one day I would see my kids again. I had to stay optimistic.

Not long after, Margaret's second husband ended up throwing Suzanne, Lorraine and Michael out of his house and they were taken into care. They stayed with my sister and my brother in law's relatives until they were old enough to fend for themselves. The courts wouldn't give me custody because they deemed me irresponsible as I didn't have my own home and a permanent job based in one place. I was angry at the ridiculous law system in this country and my ex. Margaret and her husband had dragged me through the courts to gain custody in the first place and now, because they had two children of their own, Margaret's husband didn't want my offspring around him any more. He was throwing them out like rubbish. I couldn't understand why my ex wife simply gave up on them and let them go into care. Still, I had no say in the matter. I was livid.

To this day I regret signing those adoption papers for Suzanne, Lorraine and Michael. But Margaret and her husband made it impossible for me to see my children and I gave up fighting for them when Social Services told the judge that the kids would be better off if Margaret's husband adopted them.

You think that you are doing what's best for your children and you follow the advice of the professionals who deal with this sort of thing day in and day out. You believe that social workers and solicitors know best, but it doesn't always turn out that way. Over the years I have tried to gain custody and frequent visiting rights to my children but the courts have always viewed me as an unreliable father, due to my job and lifestyle. I guess that if I had lived in one place, with a proper home and a good solid income I would have had more rights. I know that I was irresponsible but I never gave up trying to see any of my children and even when their mothers made it difficult to contact them I lived in hope that one day things would change. Perhaps I could have fought harder for them. That thought haunts me. Like my childhood memories though, I managed to bury my fears and simply got on with my life the only way I knew how.

In April 1981 I contacted Pontins' head office, to see if they had any vacancies for bluecoats for the coming season. I thought that they would all have been taken, but to my surprise I was offered a position at Brean Sands in Somerset. On arrival there a young lad with scruffy bleached hair charged up to me with a big smile and said "Hi, my name's Shane Richie." It was long before his days on stage and in TV soaps but he stood out in a crowd, even then. I liked his energy at once.

I used my stage name, Scott Wilde, as I thought it had more of a showbiz ring to it than Ron Sheppard.

As the season started we all took turns in doing reception duties, meeting the guests as they arrived every Saturday. It was part of Pontins' tradition, just like when I was back at Camber Sands; a cracking way to meet the girls. The men lined up behind the front desk and flashed their best smiles as the women sauntered past and later we'd discuss who had the nicest face or body, or how much we would score each one out of ten. Usually the bluecoats were hung over from the night before but it never stopped them from admiring the ladies. We weren't allowed to drink on duty but if our boss caught us with a sly vodka in our lemonades we'd say, "But a guest bought it for me, Alan. I couldn't say no. It would be rude." Not once did I or the other blues have to put their hands in their own pockets. There were many perks to being a bluecoat if you know what I mean. It was like being famous. Everyone wanted to know you and the girls couldn't get enough of us. Shane and Goss were even sharing the same girl, Gos first up to the chalet then Shane. Some of these girls make out they are older than they are. I could never share a girl like that.

I think the female staff did pretty well with the male guests, too. There were different people going in and out of staff chalets all times of the day and night. It was like musical beds.

The shock of another marriage going down the toilet faded and the party atmosphere helped deflect my attention from my personal problems. There were a lot of male staff at the camp and although I had never felt all that keen to make friends with other fellas as I got older I felt my past tenseness with men ease slightly. At holiday camps I made some wonderful friends of both sexes and during those times I thought about Frank less. I was busy having too much fun.

Every morning we were up at the crack of dawn filming our own version of 'Tizwaz', playing pranks on one another for the camera, which the guests could watch live on their TVs in their chalets each day. One morning me and the other bluecoats – Shane, Gos, Rosie, Frank and Blocks (we called one of the guys Blockhead) - all had to take our beds out onto the road, lined up alongside each other, get into bed and pretend to be asleep. And then Alan Shields, the Centre Manager, pretended to be a sergeant major and strutted about with this stick, poking us with it to get us up as his shoulder length brown hair swished about in the breeze.

"Get up you lazy lot!" he shouted. "Get up and give me 20 press ups! Now!"

The guests loved watching us mess about while they were having breakfast, but when we weren't entertaining the guests we were mainly busy pulling the women. It wasn't allowed, fraternizing with guests, but holiday camps were meat markets back in those days.

One afternoon Alan called all the male blues into his office, one by one. I was the first to be hauled in.

"Sit down, Scott." Alan was behind his desk and was fiddling with a Biro.

I did as I was told. "You look serious, Alan. What's up?" Although he was my boss, Alan wasn't all that much older than me and he could be a good laugh. When riled, he was as tough as old boots, mind you.

"You lot is what's up. That's what's bloody up again, Ron," Alan snapped in his Manchester accent.

"Huh?"

"Messing about with the female guests again. The big boss doesn't like it and I'm getting an ear bashing."

"I don't know what you mean," I said.

"Don't give me that shit, Scott. I'm not thick."

"I didn't say you were…"

"Shut up will you for once. I've got something to ask you."

"OK," I gulped.

"One of the female guests told me something very interesting last night." Alan was tapping his fingers on his desk.

"Did she?"

"Yes. Very interesting indeed, Scott…"

"OK…" I felt my face go hot; worried I'd got someone pregnant.

"She said she'd got a dose of the clap. So if any of you lot have been giving her one it means you've got it, too. Have you been having sex with a girl with long wavy brown hair and big bazookas recently?" Alan's hands were cupping imaginary breasts.

"No…"

His brown eyes were suspicious. "You sure about that?"

"Not me, Alan. You know me… I don't sleep with the guests."

He slumped back in his seat and sighed, ushering me in the direction of the door. "Get out, will you. Send the next clown in."

I wasn't sure exactly which girl he was talking about, but I was pretty certain that I hadn't slept with anyone matching the description he gave me. Although a couple of the other lads looked worried when they left Alan's office and had to take a two-week course of antibiotics to treat VD. It turned out no one actually had it, but it was just a precaution. I had my suspicions that the whole thing was a lie, made up by Alan to keep us in line and stop us messing about with the guests. For a while the guys and I did keep our trousers up, but it didn't last long. We were soon up to our old tricks, with Alan trying to come up with ingenious ways to stop us sneaking girls into our rooms.

Every night we were all up on stage, leading the way with the dancing, a little number called 'The Slosh,' which was a Pontins invention. Shane always had the kids flocking around him, as he had a special charm about him. They loved him and Blocks, a nice looking young fella with curly fair hair. Those two were constantly playing the fool on stage. The kids followed them everywhere, they were so funny. Mind you, so did the prettiest girls. If I had to place the male staff in order of popularity with the ladies it was Shane first, Blocks second, and me, I would chalk up as a third place contender. Sometimes I had to pinch myself. I felt like I was Mick Jagger or someone of that ilk.

Female guests were fair game, but I told myself not to get too familiar with the staff when working on the camps. It would have been awkward if it didn't work out. I also kept reminding myself not to get involved in any kind of a relationship. I had had three wives and another divorce was under way. My track record with women was appalling.

But then I spotted Kathy working in the cafeteria. She was slim with shoulder length blonde hair and I fancied her at once. After introducing myself while she piled sausages and beans onto my plate one morning I spent most nights sleeping in her chalet, in a single bed with a paper thin mattress. It all seemed very romantic to me and as we lay there in the darkness, cuddled up after our first time together, Kathy said in her strong Cornish accent, "Aye 'ad a feeling I'd be losing my virginity 'ere."

"That's nice," I said and kissed her nose.

Kathy's blue eyes peered into mine and she smiled. I thought how lovely she looked with her hair strewn all over the pillow.

"Aye really likes you, Scott," she said.

I gave her bum a squeeze. "I like you, too."

"Maybe I'll go on the pill." Kathy was a sensible girl.

The other bluecoats constantly played pranks on us, which we would stumble across when we went back to Kathy's place after work. Blocks, Shane or one of the others thought it hilarious to put plastic dog poop or y-fronts streaked with Marmite under the bed covers. Kathy and I didn't care; we were too busy falling in love.

We'd been an item for a month when, cuddling up in bed again, she said, "Scott, d'you think we's should be gettin' engaged, like?"

I thought about it for a few moments. Oh dear that word again. This is my problem I don't like to say no and hurt people's feelings.

"Yeah, why not?" I answered.

18

I told Kathy that I was waiting for the divorce from Lesley to be finalised and I talked constantly about Lee and Craig, but I didn't let on about my other wives or children. Whenever Kathy met my parents I warned them not to mention Margaret or Jeanette or get the wedding photo albums out. Once a marriage was over Mum took out the old photographs from the album and replaced the shots with pictures of my new bride. While I waited for my latest divorce to come through Dad never tired of saying, "Now you've finished with this one, Ron, can I have her?"

Kathy's Cornish accent was very noticeable and she said things like, "Where they begone then?" and "What thee be doing?" Half the time I couldn't understand what on earth she was saying but I found it endearing and was quite keen on her. So I was nervous when it came to meeting her family for the first time. I was wary of stepping foot in Chester because of Lesley's dad still being on the warpath so I was anxious about girls' relatives taking a liking to me. Plus, Kathy was only 18 and I was 32. I was expecting a knuckle sandwich from her stepdad. But this time it was the mother I had to watch out for.

It was a Friday evening and I was on my break when I ran back to my room to spruce myself up for my first meeting with Kathy's parents. They were driving up from Cornwall especially. I knew that Kathy was excited about our relationship and really wanted her parents to like me, so it was important that I made a good first impression. I had a quick wash and slicked on some Brylcreem and then I walked towards the cafeteria, a spacious room that was set up like a proper restaurant and echoed with the sound of cutlery rattling and people talking and laughing. Kathy was there, waiting for me, sitting at one of the round tables that the guests' and staff ate their meals at. She was in a summery white sundress and looked so pretty. Alan, Shane and Blocks were sitting at a table nearby and winked at me when I walked in. They knew that I was about to be "interrogated by the in-laws" as Blocks called it.

"Her dad's gonna beat you up, Scott," guffawed Blocks as he tucked into his dinner. He waved his fork in my direction. "You better watch it, mate!"

"Thanks, mate," I grimaced, taking the seat next to Kathy. "Alright, love?" I said and kissed her on the cheek.

"Where they be? It be gettin' late." Kathy looked as nervous as me. I was her first serious boyfriend so introducing me to her folks was a big thing for her.

"Don't worry, Kath. They'll be here soon."

"There they be! Woo-hoo!" Kathy sprung up from her seat and waved at three people – a blonde woman, followed by a skinny little bloke in a flat cap. And behind Kathy's mother and stepfather was her grandmother, a tiny lady carrying a big handbag.

I stood up and grinned as the trio walked towards us smiling and it didn't escape my notice that Kathy's mother was quite an attractive lady, probably in her late thirties or early forties at most.

Other bluecoats were hovering around by now and they were all sniggering in our direction and pulling daft faces. It made me more anxious than ever.

Kathy had already told me that she was close to her stepdad and that he worked down the clay mines. It struck me that he looked quite healthy for a miner. I assumed that they were all pasty-looking from being underground all the time. I also noticed that he had decent arm muscles and I hoped that he wasn't going to take an instant dislike to me. Fathers could be very protective of their daughters, I reminded myself. I needn't have worried about him though.

"Aye, it's you there, is it, Scott?" Kathy's Mum barged ahead. She was a slim lady with a strong Cornish accent and she came at me like she was running for the last bus. I was quite surprised and took a few steps backwards. The other blues were silent and open-mouthed as Barbara suddenly waved a fist in the air and shouted: "So you be the one who took my daughter's virginity!"

Barbara's face was serious while she stood, hands on hips, chin jutted forward. You could have heard a mouse fart in that cafeteria. Kathy was looking at the floor, her stepdad's face was unreadable and assorted bluecoats hovered in the background, staring at me silently for a reaction.

"Um," I said.

"Mum..." murmured Kathy. Her grandmother didn't flinch.

Barbara's expression showed that she meant business and I was just about to explain that I loved her daughter and that my intentions were honourable when Barbara slapped me gently on the cheek a couple of times.

"What was it like then, Scott?"

"Pardon?" I wasn't sure I'd heard her correctly.

"Did ye enjoy it?" Barbara's eyebrows arched.

I didn't know what to say, other than, "Um, yes, very nice, thank you, Mrs. Batchelor."

"I like he!" she laughed loudly and patted my cheek again.

The blues surrounding us broke into rapturous applause and they were laughing and jeering so much that guests also began to flock around us to see what was going on.

"Look at his face!" cackled Barbara and she nudged Kathy, who blushed.

"Oh, Mum," she said, and her eyes rolled.

Shane's and my favourite place to work was the Cabaret Club, which was set apart from the main ballroom and we both introduced the singers and comedians each night. Shane loved to introduce Gary Wilmot, who was a regular visiting act at Pontins and one of the nicest men in showbiz.

One day Jan Kennedy, our entertainment executive, came to watch the show and I was a bag of nerves when I spotted her in the front row in her smart suit and tidy blonde hairdo. She had a reputation for being nice but tough so I hoped she would approve of what she saw. While I stood on stage, rattling out jokes and making the audience feel welcome, I looked at her face. She didn't appear to be annoyed but then again she didn't seem to be overwhelmed with laughter either. I guessed she was simply being professional.

A week later Alan tracked me down at work while I was helping the other staff to blow up balloons in the ballroom.

"Scott, Jan's on the phone. She wants a word," he said gravely.

I gulped. My first reaction was one of panic, wondering if she'd heard about my flings with girls in the past or if she disapproved of me seeing Kathy. Maybe she hadn't enjoyed my impressions when she watched the show?

"What does she want?" I asked.

Alan looked uninterested and was already wandering off. "I reckon she's probably going to sack you."

"Oh God!" I shrieked. As Alan walked away I could see his shoulders shaking and he had his hand to his mouth. I followed him back to his office to take the call, feeling utterly sick. But when I picked up the receiver I was pleasantly surprised; she praised my talents and said she had heard only good things about me from Alan and the guests. She said I was perfect Entertainments Manager material and offered me the role at Tower Beach in Prestatyn, North Wales, which was a shock as I knew it was the oldest and biggest Pontins of all, holding 3,000 guests. I was flattered and immediately accepted, although I did tell her that Kathy and I were engaged and I was worried about leaving her behind. Jan offered her the role of children's auntie, which I accepted on Kathy's behalf. After the call I ran out of a grinning Alan's office in a state of excitement and found Kathy in the canteen.

"Looks like we're off to Wales, Kathy!" I cried, hugging her while filling her in about Jan's offer.

"Children's auntie! I'd be lovin' that job!" Kathy said.

"One thing though..." A sad thought struck me.

"What's wrong?" asked Kathy.

"We better say goodbye to the others. We go in a few days."

"A few days! Well I be blowed..." Kathy looked stunned.

I was over the moon about the new role but the blues in Brean were a great team and I knew I would miss them all – Shane and Blocks especially. Two days before Kathy and I left for Tower Beach, a surprise party was put on for us in the ballroom and even the guests were in on it. We had so many cards and presents from the other blues that Kathy and I were a little tearful when it came to saying goodbye. Alan showed up at the party and said, "Scott, you know where I am if you need any advice." He gave me a manly hug and patted me on the shoulder.

"Thanks, boss. You've been great," I said, trying not to snivel. Everyone gave us a hug and that night in bed Kathy and I discussed the future.

After Kathy and I dropped our cases off in our chalets at Tower Beach, North Wales, she went off to find her co-workers I headed to the ballroom because I had been informed there was a big do on in there and I was the one to oversee everything. I went up to the bar and introduced myself to the staff as the new Entertainments Manager. They seemed like a chirpy lot as they re-filled the spirits' optics with litre bottles of spirits and polished the wooden top of the bar. A couple of them were dashing about, playing frisbee with the beermats but I was always one for the staff having a laugh while they worked so I let them get on with it.

As it was my first weekend at the place I was keen to make an impression although I was a little intimidated by Tower Beach's reputation and size. The place was packed with holidaymakers but I noticed that they looked a little different to the usual types you find in camps like Pontins. There were no women done up to the nines in high heels and layers of slap or men wearing Union Jack shorts, socks and sandals. There were no kids running about, dropping ice cream down their t-shirts either. I thought it odd, but assumed that the Welsh were simply a more demurely dressed bunch. I reasoned that perhaps they let their hair down when it got late into the night.

At 8pm the band was ready to roll and the glitter ball was casting slivers of light on the walls and ceiling. The DJ was playing 'Angelo' by The Brotherhood of Man and I felt a massive surge of excitement as I glanced around the venue. This was my place. I was in charge. I was going to make it the best holiday camp ever and as far as I was concerned this was my grand debut. It was like someone had made me manager of the Albert Hall, I was so charged with adrenalin. I couldn't wait for the place to fill up and to introduce myself to the guests. I thought maybe I'd get up on stage and throw in a few of my best impressions, once people had had a few snifters.

Twenty minutes later I scanned the room again and glanced at the entrance of the ballroom. Two women came in and joined a group of men in patterned jumpers.

An old lady sauntered up to me. "Are you the boss?"

"Yes I am. How can I help you, my lovely?" I chirped.

"The music's too loud! Can you turn it down?" she huffed. She then turned on her heel and sat on her own and took out her knitting from her handbag.

I counted nine people in the whole place. I followed a man in a woolly poncho to the bar and saw him order tomato juice, not the usual gin and tonics or pints of lager that the clientele usually knocked back by as if their lives depended on it. I'd seen more atmosphere in a library.

"What's going on, Malcolm?" I asked one of the staff who was pacing up and down behind the bar, looking bored. "Is this place always like this?" I was worried. Had I made a mistake, leaving the mayhem of Brean Sands and coming to Prestatyn?

"Nah, but no one told us up front who was coming this weekend otherwise we wouldn't have gone to so much fuss, what with the streamers and balloons and stuff," he said and let out a sigh. "900 of them booked in for the whole weekend... *great...*"

"What d'you mean?" I asked.

"This lot don't like partying, drinking or enjoying themselves by the looks of it," replied Malcolm.

"But I booked a top comedian for later... and a belly dancer... and..." I began.

"Waste of time if you ask me..."

"Huh?" I felt deflated.

"This lot aren't into fun, like I said." Malcolm was polishing a beer pump with a tea towel.

"Where are they from?" I asked.

"They're the British Society for Knitting and Tapestry. This is their annual weekend shindig."

Although we had our own little chalets, Kathy and I pretty much lived together in one. Staff weren't meant to fraternize at work but we thought that as our wedding was imminent it didn't matter too much. Kathy was enjoying her job working with the kids and I loved my new role and was in charge of 15 bluecoats. I also decided to approach Jan Kennedy and the other main managers with an idea.

There was an empty cabaret room right next door to the ballroom, which got packed in the evenings, so I suggested that we opened the other room and put on cabarets, like I used to at Brean. Management weren't keen on the idea at first but eventually gave in and within a month I was bringing in 1200 bookings a week. The shows I was arranging were a hit and more visiting cabaret were secured, real big star names. I booked The Graham Passé Show Band, a brilliant four piece that were an outstanding success with the guests. Graham was also a presenter with BBC Radio Stoke. Another visiting act was The Minitones, otherwise known to everyone as Kenny and Frank. Considering they were both only three foot tall they had great presence on stage when they sang and cracked jokes in between songs.

The club turned out to be such a success and word soon got around, meaning that numerous cabaret acts on the circuit wanted to appear there, including Jackie Scott, Winston, Vince Earl, Gary Wilmot and Carol Lee Scott, who stopped appearing on the holiday camp circuit when she went on to bigger things, playing 'Grotbags', the green-faced witch on children's TV. They were all fabulous but I will confess my favourites were Don D. Williams and his wife Doreen. Don would impersonate Rod Stewart, belting out his hits while wearing leopard skin tights and a blond wig. I still see Don and his wife to this day.

One of my favourite memories regarding Tower Beach was playing in the same team as World Cup hero Sir Geoff Hurst. I always loved my football but wasn't one for sitting in front of the TV for hours, watching it. It was an FA coaching week, a chance for youngsters to be coached by top professionals and all us blues joined in, kicking balls about the whole place with the kids.

Time went by so quickly and we were now into our final weekend of the season, and there was a lot of talk about going out with a big bang amongst the staff. But we spoke too soon. It was time for the British Pool Association Championships, where pool pub teams would compete with each other for the UK title. It was dubbed 'The Battle of the Balls'. On the first day of the event over 2000 supporters and the players from pubs all over the country arrived at Tower Beach on coaches. I couldn't believe my eyes when I saw hordes of drunken men jump off the vehicles and urinate in the road, in the fountain, up walls, down paths, and even where they stood, while singing rude songs. As soon as I heard the lyrics and saw the type of clientele that were exiting the coaches a tingle of fear shot through me. The cabaret acts I'd booked for that night were The Minitones and a singer from the West Indies called Winston, who sang traditional songs from his homeland. My stomach did a back-flip when I saw a bald bloke with a tattooed neck take a swig from a can of beer, burp in his mate's face and shout, "C'mon, Tez, ya bastard! Let's find the fuckin' bar!"

I found out from one of the coach drivers that these men had been drinking for over 24 hours, so I gave the female bluecoats the weekend off and warned them not to go out alone at night. Then I warned Kathy to stay in her chalet with the curtains shut. Call me dramatic but I felt uneasy, what with so much liquor-soused testosterone in one place.

The ballroom was heaving that night with drunken men shouting at one another and doing moonies or singing football songs. I felt sick. I hated big groups of men at the best of times, but these guys looked like savages to me. I could see Winston at the side of the stage, warming up his voice before he went on. I thought he looked calm considering the state of the audience and it wasn't even 9pm.

"Winston, mate, I don't think you should go on tonight," I said. He was dressed in an evening suit and dickey bow.

"It's OK, Ron. I've seen worse in my time," he replied, shrugging.

I wasn't sure I believed him but it was his choice and as he walked on stage the place fell silent.

Oh, bloody hell... I thought, and waited.

But I needn't have fretted because as soon as Winston was two sentences into his first track the audience went wild, cheering him on. They loved his melodic voice and gave him a standing ovation at the end of his act, whistling and stamping their feet. And when The Minitones came off stage they got the same treatment, too. I guess I had been too hasty in my judgment. These men looked like trouble but they were just out for a good time, nothing else. When the bluecoats waved them off on their coaches on the Monday morning we all agreed it was a successful end to the summer season.

A few days later Kathy went home to see her parents and I stayed on at the camp, helping management with the auditions to find new bluecoats for the next season. When I see 'The X-Factor' on TV now it reminds me of those times. I lost count of the amount of girls who sang 'I will Survive'. There must have been at least 25 wannabe Gloria Gaynor's every day of those bluecoat trials and each girl had bigger hair and more make-up than the last.

I loved being a judge and my take on it was that as long as people could hold a tune, had a good personality and were reasonably okay looking they were in. I was no Simon Cowell.

Kathy and I had decided that we wanted a March wedding and the day soon arrived in 1981. We booked a little church in the pretty town of St. Austell in Cornwall and Shane had agreed to be my best man. The evening before the wedding I was a nervous wreck, especially when there was no sign of him. All of the other bluecoats had made it to the hotel where the guests were staying and said they had no idea where he was. Frantic, I ran to the nearest phone box and rang Shane's mother, who told me he had flu and couldn't make it. Shane said that he would try to come in the morning but his mother said she didn't want him leaving his bedroom and getting worse. I hoped for a miracle. In even more of a state after a sleepless night, I ran to the church the following morning and found my brother-in-law John, who was standing next to my sister, in his best back suit and tie again. He had heard the commotion amongst us bluecoats, about Shane still not making the ceremony, and was eyeing me warily as I walked up to him.

"I'm not doing it again, Ron," he warned, holding the flats of his hands up as if to keep me away. "You promised me last time, no more bloody weddings."

"This is my last one," I pleaded. "Go on, John..."

He shook his head. "You said - *no more weddings!*"

"I haven't got time for this!" I shrieked, spotting Kathy getting out of her stepdad's car in her big white dress. "Who wants to be my best man? I'll give anyone who does it a tenner!" I spun around, looking at the men in the gathering crowd of guests while waving a ten pound note about. In the end James, one of the bluecoats, did the honours and a good job he managed, too. He refused my money as well which I thought was nice of him.

So, dressed in the same suit as I wore for my wedding to Lesley seven years before, I stood at the alter waiting for my fiancé to join me. As I watched her walking down the aisle in her finery I thought how pretty she looked. Kathy let go of her stepfather's arm and stood beside me at the alter. Organ music played in the background and I felt lucky to be marrying such a beautiful girl. I caught my mother's eye. She smiled. I was determined to make her proud of me. I took Kathy's hand and the vicar began to speak.

This time it's going to be different, I promised myself.

19

There was no time for a honeymoon because the Monday after the wedding I was holed up in a Manchester theatre for the bluecoat audition process again, so Kathy stayed in Cornwall with her parents and I got on with my job.

One day Jan Kennedy and her husband Jim, who was also one of the big bosses, took me to one side during a break and said they had a proposition for me.

"Fred wants you for Little Canada, Scott," said Jan, sipping her coffee. "What d'you reckon?"

I wasn't sure I'd heard straight – that Sir Fred Pontin actually wanted me to run the entertainment programme at the best holiday camp on the Isle of Wight. It was where I had begun my career and I had always missed the island.

"Really?" I asked.

"It's a great opportunity," Jim smiled. "Billy Crush has been entertainments manager there for eight years with his old time musical shows, but it's time to modernise. Fred thinks you're the man to do it."

Billy Crush had been my boss when I worked at Pontins in 1971. I didn't need to be asked twice. I accepted the job right away – on one proviso; that Shane Richie was to be my number two. We were a team and I knew how great he was with audiences. If anyone could help me make a success of the place it was him.

"It's a deal!" grinned Jan. She hugged me and Jim shook my hand.

It was an exciting time for me professionally and personally as I had also regained contact with my two sons Lee and Craig who were five and three. Their mother Lesley had remarried and made it clear that she wanted me out of the picture so that they could bond with their stepfather. I was not pleased that I had been pushed out yet again and I had called and asked to see my children many times, but I hadn't seen them for a few years. Lesley's father was still out for my blood too and she reminded me not to set foot in Chester. I had no intention of going back there, however I didn't see why I should be kept out of my kids' lives. So, Lesley had relented and agreed that they could come and stay with me for a weekend. When Lesley drove up in the car and dropped the boys off I had to hold back the tears. They had grown up so much. After some shyness from them both the three of us had a great time on the beach and the fairground rides. When they went home I sat in my chalet for hours wondering when I would see them again. I knew that my strained relationship with my ex and her family meant that it would be hard to gain proper, ongoing access. I had to accept what time I was offered and get on with my life. I found it incredibly hard to deal with the fact that I wasn't a full time father. I felt empty without my children.

In April 1981 Kathy, Shane and I took the ferry from Southampton to the Isle of Wight and caught a coach to Little Canada. Shane was very excited during the journey and Kathy was pleased because she had landed the job as children's auntie. When we got there one of the staff showed us around the site and the three of us looked at one another with appreciation as we took in the log cabins set out in neat rows, named after places in Canada, like Ontario. The cabins were spread around woods that lead down to River Creek.

"Nice place," whistled Shane.

"Not bad," I agreed.

We had been at Little Canada for less than two months when we had some good news to share with the bluecoats during one of our team meetings.

"We're going to have a baby!" I announced, with my arm around my new wife. Kathy had taken three home pregnancy tests and all came out positive. We were elated and wanted to tell everyone straight away.

"Congratulations, Scott, Kathy!" Shane sprang up from his seat and ran to us, giving us both a big hug. "Can I be godfather?"

Kathy giggled. "We 'aven't thought that far yet!"

Shane was in one of his excitable moods now and his finger shot up in the air. "I know! Let's celebrate everyone! I'll buy champagne!" He ran off laughing and came back a few minutes later with a bottle of champers in an ice bucket, and glasses.

"Only the best bubbly for my mates!" he cried, popping it open and sharing it out among the staff. "Cheers Scott, Kathy! Here's to your new nipper!"

I found out later from the barmaid that he hadn't paid for the champagne, so I gave her the money.

Poor Kathy suffered from terrible morning sickness and had to give up work. She spent most of her time with her head hovering over the toilet. She even had to be sent to hospital because she became so dehydrated.

Shane and I went to visit her in the ward. Kathy looked pale and very small as she lay in her bed.

"Alright, Kath?" I asked and handed her some flowers which she put on the cabinet until a nurse could find a vase.

"Here ya go." Shane pecked her on the cheek and thrust a wilted bouquet in her hand. I knew he had pinched the sorry-looking shrubs from the flowerbeds surrounding the camp just before we got on the bus to the hospital.

"Thanks, Shane…" Kathy smiled weakly.

"Ah, before I forget!" Shane handed her an envelope.

Kathy opened the card and read it. She glanced up at Shane and said "Erm, thanks." I leant over and studied the card. It had 'With sympathy' embossed on the front and a picture of an angel playing a harp.

"That's a card you send out when someone snuffs it!" I said to Shane.

"I know but it was all the shop had," he shrugged and then smiled brightly. "But I thought it still works as it's showing sympathy for all the times Kathy's spewed her guts up…"

He had a point.

Because of Kathy's condition I decided that Shane and I should split the shifts between us. When we were at Brean Sands one of Shane's specialities was dressing up as a tramp, with a bottle in hand, scraggy old clothes, wellies and manure spread on his face, so he smelled terrible. We would then kid the guests he was a homeless man who often followed people about on site, begging for money, but we said that they should ignore him. One Sunday the blues ran a ramble over neighbouring countryside and 300 guests turned up for it. Halfway through Shane turned up in his tramp gear, liquor bottle swaying and stinking of cow dung.

"Anyone got any spare change?" he sniffed, holding a moth-eaten gloved hand out. "I ain't had a bite to eat in six days."

Soon the ramble ventured over the nearby Warner's Holiday camp site and the staff got annoyed when they saw a tramp mooching about, begging for money from their guests, as well as ours. They called the police. Later that day two coppers turned up to speak to me. The staff at Warner's and the police were suspicious that it was one of our gags as there was great rivalry between holiday camps.

"No, it was nothing to do with us," I said.

"You positive?" asked one of the officers.

"We don't have tramps at this site, officer," I replied. "It's a reputable establishment. But if I do see him I'll let you know." I could hear giggling from the blues standing behind me at reception.

"Well we'll leave it at that then," said the middle aged copper suspiciously. "C'mon, Gus." He motioned for his colleague to follow him to the squad car that was parked out front of the building.

The following Saturday our new clubhouse, the Mounties Retreat, was to open. A large percentage of the place was decorated with logs, in fitting with the whole Canadian theme and wooden picnic tables filled the room, in wait for all the guests who would turn up to see the show. That night had been planned as a grand affair because the big bosses were coming for a visit and my parents were also arriving by coach for a week-long holiday the very same evening. I was introducing the cabaret and was keen to make a good impression on everyone. But just as I was waiting at the entrance area for my parents' coach to turn up, I spotted a squad car parking and saw the same two police officers get out and walk towards me.

"Evening, officers," I said. "How can I help?"

"We came to find out if you'd seen that tramp again," said the older of the two coppers.

"Nope, I'm just standing here, waiting for my parents and the main management team to turn up," I said.

The policemen looked at one another and then smiled at me. "I've got an idea," one of them said.

"Oh yeah?" I replied.

He dangled his handcuffs in front of him. "Why don't you put these cuffs on and see your parents' reactions when they get here? Give them a little surprise?"

I thought it was a thoroughly hilarious plan. "Ha ha! What a good idea! Go on then!" I held my wrists out, with the other blues behind me in stitches. The officer slapped the cuffs on me, laughed and walked off with his partner.

"Hey, where you going?" I shouted, running after them, arms outstretched. Any minute the big brass of the company was going to turn up and it was my job to show them a good time, kicking it all off with a welcome speech in front of hundreds of guests, too.

One of the officers stopped and leant on the top of the squad car. "You must think I'm daft. I know you lot were behind that tramp trick last week." Then the two of them got in the car and drove off.

I ran after them shouting, "Come back!"

Shane was practically on the floor, he was laughing so much. "You're a right burke!" he cried, pointing at me.

I spent all night in those cuffs, with Shane following constantly behind me, shouting out, "Scott, there's a time and a place to get your handcuffs out!"

My parents found it all amusing but I felt daft having to get up on stage and introduce the acts like that. The officer who cuffed me came back at midnight with the keys and let me go.

I was dying to get my own back on Shane so the following Sunday, just before the ramble, I spoke to Ken Bruce about my plan and he gave his blessing. The two security guards on shift were new and didn't know Shane so I told them we had been bothered by a smelly tramp and I wanted them to throw him off the camp if he showed up. So, when Shane staggered through the site, ready to join the ramble in his tatty gear the security guards grabbed him in front of all the guests and marched him off the grounds, with Shane shouting, "C'mon, lads! It's me – Shane!"

For hours Shane was left outside the main gate, pleading his case to anyone who passed by and would listen. Eventually Ken Bruce went up to the security guards and told them who Shane was.

"You bastard," Shane said to me later.

It was 1982 and the Canberra was returning from the Falklands war. She was due to pass by the camp at 7.30am and the big boss, Mr. Bruce, asked Shane and me to escort people down to the beach at 7.00am to give the ship a cheer as she passed. We had a full camp of over 400 guests joining us on the seafront to greet the ship, so the air was full of excitement. It was very foggy and we could hardly see a thing, but we heard this loud foghorn getting closer and closer. Then we saw the side of a white ship edging through the mist. Everyone immediately started cheering and waving.

Shane jumped up and down. "There she is everyone!" he shouted, pointing into the distance. "There's the Canberra!"

After a minute or so one of the guests suddenly shouted, "That's not the Canberra!"

It turned out to be the Isle of Wight car ferry coming into Wootton near us. The Canberra had already glided past but we hadn't spotted her, due to the dense fog. So, everyone had got up extra early just to see an old car ferry go by. Shane and I thought it was hilarious, but some of the guests didn't see the humorous side and complained to Ken Bruce. We got a ticking off from Ken but we were used to it by now and just agreed with everything he said.

We were all looking forward to the end of season as it had been a long hard summer and Shane asked me if he could do his own cabaret act in the Mounties Retreat the following week. He usually doubled up with someone else but I knew he had the talent to stand out on his own, even though I thought his singing voice needed a little work. But he was full of charm and very comical. So I gave Shane his first taste at going solo. His idol was Elvis Presley and his rendition of 'The Wonder of You' was impressive. I laughed myself silly when he walked on stage wearing sunglasses and a pair of dark tights pulled over his head, with one of the other blues leading the way. He then sat at keyboard and sang a Stevie Wonder song, while doing all the actions. He was brilliant and the audience lapped it up.

One night after his act, he told me that two girls wanted to see us in their chalet. Kathy had gone to bed.

"I don't know, Shane…" I said.

"It's OK, they only want a chat," he replied.

I had no intention of being unfaithful to Kathy but saw no harm in talking to women. "Alright if you're sure…"

The four of us went to the girls' chalet and he and one girl disappeared into the bathroom, leaving me with the other one, who was already in bed and beckoning me to join her. I think she might have been naked although I'm not sure. She certainly had no top on. I stood there in a quandary while I could hear all sorts of rude noises coming out of the bathroom, followed suddenly by Shane's shocked voice: "What the heck?!"

Not having put the bathroom light on, Shane had jumped into a bath full of freezing cold water with only his socks on and got tangled up in the girls' underwear and tights that had been soaking in the tub. It put a dampener on the girl's passion and he had been asked to leave. As the two of us walked back to our chalets I couldn't stop laughing. I laughed so much I got gut ache.

"Shut up, Scott," said Shane, frowning. "It ain't that funny."

"Yes it is," I said. "Serves you right."

Kathy suffered with sickness throughout her whole pregnancy so she was glad to go into labour. Our daughter Kelly was born on 22nd February 1982 and when we got back to the holiday centre we were in for a shock. Ken Bruce told us both that he wasn't insured to have babies on the grounds and that we had to move out. He was happy to let me stay but Kathy and Kelly had to go. There was no way I was splitting my family up as I didn't want to risk losing Kathy, so I agreed to part company with Pontins. I was gutted as I loved my job there. Ken let us stay until the end of the season which was nearing anyway and on the last day I was sad to say goodbye to everyone, especially Shane, but we kept in touch.

After staying in a friend's bedsit for a while, eventually the council gave us a two bedroom ground floor flat in Ryde, which faced a main road. It was reasonably modern with lounge cum diner, storage heaters and a small back yard in which to hang washing, but Kathy didn't like the kitchen because she said it was just about big enough to swing a mouse in. It wouldn't have mattered if we'd been given a palace though; Kathy wanted to go back to Cornwall because she missed living near her family. I liked being on the island so it was the cause of some disharmony between us. Also, we were together all the time, whereas before we had both had jobs to keep us busy. Looking back, Kathy and I weren't as close as we had seemed when we were living in the camps. There were lots of distractions around us and when we were in a house together with a small baby 24/7 the cracks began to show.

"I wants us to move to Cornwall. I hate it 'ere!" Kathy yelled at me again.

"We've got a nice house here, Kath." I thought she was being selfish. She had never mentioned wanting to live near her parents before we were married.

"I be bored livin' 'ere!" she shouted.

"Well take up a hobby then!" I said.

"Like what?"

"I dunno… what do you like?" I asked.

"I likes livin' in Cornwall!"

"That's not a hobby! What about a part time job?" I suggested. Her face went bright red.

"Aye just 'ad a baby! You 'spect me ta go down the clay mine with me stepdad?"

I didn't want Kathy to get a job but it was the first thing that had come into my brain.

"No, I just want you to be happy here," I sighed.

"Well, I ain't!"

The fact that I couldn't work as I was attending hospital again because my back problem was getting worse didn't help matters between Kathy and me. While at Pontins I had fallen off stage in the middle of doing one of my Norman Wisdom impressions and it had aggravated my old injury. I was 35 and having steroid epidurals every three months for the pain. I got myself a job on the local buses, as a conductor, but that didn't help my health situation, so I had to give that up and go on the sick again. Kathy wasn't impressed.

My specialist informed me that I needed more back surgery because I could hardly stand, let alone walk. I was admitted to Southampton General Hospital for my operation, where I remained for a month. This was because of leaking spinal fluid, which was dangerous and could have caused brain damage. The doctors thought I would have to go back to theatre again if the leakage didn't stop within 24 hours. Fortunately it did - after spending the whole day literally tipped upside down on my bed, so the fluid could drain back. During all this Kathy never brought Kelly to see me once and Kathy herself didn't visit me either. The relatives' accommodation was available to her and was quite nice, only it didn't interest her. I asked her to come many times but there was always some excuse. I was deeply hurt that she didn't care about me or my welfare any more. Laying in that hospital bed it hit me that my fourth marriage was over. Now, I think that Kathy was too young to be entering into a serious relationship and marriage. She was only 18 when we met.

I had too much time to think in that ward and my mind wandered back to my childhood, in Frank's house, with him touching me. Had he turned me into the person I was today, I wondered? Was that why I was so useless with women? I had never been one for self pity though and I was well aware by then that I was better off emotionally when I was with someone. Being alone wasn't good for me.

It was because of this flaw in my character that I got to know a nurse called Janice. She was an in-patient herself with a serious bladder problem and we became good friends, although it hadn't escaped my attention that she was attractive, with long blond hair and nice legs. She knitted me a jumper and helped feed me.

Janice was discharged from hospital before me but she travelled from her home in Bridport to see me every weekend, when she stayed in the relatives' accommodation. It was where we made love for the first time. I know I had been a joker in the past but I respected my marriage vows to Kathy and wanted it to work. It was not my intention to have an affair, however much I was attracted to Janice. But Kathy had made it clear that she wasn't interested in me any more and I craved the comfort of a woman.

Soon I was discharged and taken by ambulance back to the Isle of Wight, to the main hospital first, and then home a week later. Kathy was there and I knew at once that she wasn't pleased to see me. She sat on the sofa with Kelly on her lap and glared at the floor. I was on crutches and slowly made my way over to kiss my daughter. It was great to see her again and she gave me a huge smile and cried, "Daddy!"

"I don't want you 'ere," Kathy quickly blurted, her expression cold as she looked up at me.

"What?" I asked.

"Aye bin 'ere on my own a while an' that's the way I wants it to stay," she snapped. "Go." She motioned her head towards the door.

However hard I tried to persuade her to let me stay, she became more determined that she wanted me out. So within two days of being discharged from hospital I was on my way back to my sister's and out of Kathy's life. She then went straight to Cornwall and started divorce proceedings. It wasn't long before she was back with the boyfriend she went out with before me and it was arranged for me to visit my daughter through our solicitors.

Kathy started making excuses so that I couldn't see Kelly. One weekend I went all the way to Cornwall on the train and when I got there Kathy refused to let me see my daughter, going against the agreement that was made by the solicitors. I stood at her front door, glanced up to the bedroom window and saw my little Kelly crying and waving. She was looking forward to coming out with me. We used to go to the movies or to the beach for the day if the weather was nice, but Kathy wouldn't budge so I returned to my sister's place in London and hoped that she would see sense at some point.

I couldn't believe that I was being stopped from seeing yet another child of mine. It was so frustrating. I think that fathers today have more rights, although I do know of cases where men have had to endure many years of painful and expensive court cases, even to see their children every other weekend. I couldn't afford the best lawyers and when it came down to it, on paper I was a hopeless candidate for seeking joint custody.

Mine and Kathy's divorce came through and I was a free agent, so Janice and I picked up where we left off for a short while.

The battle with Kathy for access over Kelly was ongoing and out of the blue I had a letter from a social worker from the family court in Cornwall, telling me that Kathy had remarried and that she wanted me to sign papers giving permission for Kathy's new husband to adopt Kelly. I refused but soon I had a visit from Social Services, who put a lot of pressure on me, telling me and the agencies involved that this was what Kelly wanted, which I didn't believe for one minute. I still refused to sign the papers. The court declared that it was in my daughter's best interests to be adopted by Kathy's husband. Determined not to lose my daughter, I continued to stand firm, but in the end I couldn't overrule a judge who eventually made the final order in my absence. I received a letter telling me the heartbreaking news. Now I had lost my lovely Kelly as well.

20

In 1985 I got a job as a bingo caller for Corals in Kingston. Janice and I split up after while; partly because my mother was none too impressed with my love life by then and was snappy with Janice the first time they met. I doubt Janice would have been a long term girlfriend but Mum's frosty reception put her off getting involved and we drifted apart. I couldn't blame my mother. She quite liked Kathy and was fed up with me bringing different girls home to meet her and my dad. Her patience was wearing thin and she wanted me to choose a nice girl, stick with her and bring up the children together; all under one roof just as she and Dad had. How I wished I could have given her her wish. She and my father had been together for well over half a century.

"When you get fed up with this one, Ron, can I have her?" Dad asked. He always said that the old jokes were the best ones.

It was just as well that Mum didn't come to visit me at work because I was up to my old tricks again, chatting up the customers. I cracked jokes in between calling the bingo numbers out and dressed up in different costumes, often doing my Norman Wisdom impression. It had struck me a fair few years before that women love funny men so I used my silliness on stage to my advantage. I was staying in a bed and breakfast and I often took girls back there.

Luckily my experiences with Frank never put me off sleeping with girls as I didn't correlate sexual abuse with my strong attraction and enthusiasm for sex with women. The two were worlds apart. I had always had a healthy interest in the opposite sex which didn't seem to wane as I got older. My reasoning then was that I was single so I may as well make the most of my popularity. I had no intention of looking for a new long term relationship and as for marriage, well, forget it. I came to the conclusion that I wasn't the marrying type; that I should keep well away from register offices and churches - for good.

However, I soon forgot about all that and it was while I was at Corals I met Sharon, a well built girl with a strong Cockney accent.

"I can't believe I didn't win nuffin' again!" she huffed during one of our first conversations. "I come 'ere twice a week an' all I ever won was a bleedin' tenner!"

My eyes were dazzled by her blue eye shadow, pink lipstick and lurid fur jacket with shoulder pads. I was at the side of the stage after the bingo game and was about to go to the bar for a drink, so I offered to buy her one, too.

"OK, love, I'll 'ave a brandy an' coke," she said. "Then I better get going."

"Where d'you live?" I asked.

"Not far, but I don't like traveling too late 'cos there's perverts everywhere."

Although Sharon was attractive, with long brown hair and had a no nonsense air about her that I admired, I don't think I was blown away by her. But I was keen enough to move in with her in her tidy two-bedroom flat within weeks. It was a great improvement on the B&B where I was renting a room. Several months later she was pregnant.

"I think we better get married then, love I said," after she had been to the doctor's and had had the news confirmed.

"Erm, OK, said Sharon. Might be a good idea," I agreed.

We had a quick ceremony in Wandsworth register office in the late summer of 1986, when Sharon was seven months gone. Her dress was tightly stretched over her bump I was worried it might split at the seams, but she looked nice, I thought.

During a week's honeymoon in Jersey, Sharon had morning sickness so we couldn't do much, apart from drive around the place, looking at the scenery, which didn't take up much of the day, it being a small island. I recall a niggling feeling, wondering what I had got myself into, even then. But, as always, I had acted without thinking and I told myself that Sharon was a lovely lady and we were going to be happy together, what with a baby on the way.

My back injury was still causing me discomfort, so I got an office job with British Rail, at Victoria Station in London. I was also awarded Industrial Injuries Benefit for life because I couldn't continue in the entertainment business. This compensated a little for what I may have earned if I was still in the game though, but I had a disability and it was hard to accept that. British Rail then gave me a different job in the Area Manager's office, and unluckily for me I was on the front line dealing with the public's complaints, which got on my nerves.

A bloke in a suit came up to me one afternoon and said, "Why is my train not up there on the departure board?"

"Because it goes from the platform," I answered.

The man laughed and replied. "You should be on stage."

I sighed. "Funny you should say that…"

My days as an entertainer were behind me and it made me sad, knowing that. Married life with Sharon was no comparison to the excitement I felt up on stage. I was suffocated by my home and professional life. The job in the area management's office was getting stressful, so I decided to transfer to British Rail telecommunications, at the main exchange for the whole of the UK. Security was tight there as it was at the height of the IRA terror threats and bombings in the UK which were rife at London British Rail Stations. We were getting calls all the time, stating bombs were going to go off here, there and everywhere, and we had to take each threat seriously, recording all calls. The IRA used a code within their warnings so we usually knew if it was a real threat or not. It was also the time of the tragic Clapham rail crash and I remember doing two straight shifts of 18 hours that day. It was bedlam and relatives and friends were frantically calling our special hotline that had been set up.

Sharon and I had our son, Denis, and on his first birthday we were having a family party for him when there was a knock at the door. When I opened it Shane stood there with a big grin on his face and a bottle of champagne in his hand.

"Alright, me old mate?! He cried and gave me a hug.

I was so surprised to see him, as the previous week he had just made his debut on ITV's 'Sunday Palladium Live'. I thought he wouldn't be able to come as initially planned; after all he had a busy schedule following on from his successful appearance. He was going places. But that was Shane, he always kept his promise and the next thing we knew he was rolling on the floor, with all the kids jumping on him and screeching with laughter.

My back problems continued and I was having steroid epidural injections nearly every two months at Charing Cross hospital, where I was given a CT scan, to discover why I was in so much pain. No one was telling me anything, until one day a friend informed me she had seen this programme on TV, about people that had been given a myelogram, an x-ray of the spine using injected dye. She said it had left them with an incurable disease called Arachnoiditis, which caused scarring of the membranes that surround the nerve roots.

"That's like what you get isn't it, Ron?" my friend said.

At long last, there was the answer I'd been searching for. I had had two Myelograms a few years earlier to diagnose my disc problems and I was having the same symptoms as the people my friend had seen on TV. She repeated their symptoms: trouble passing water, chronic pain, a burning sensation in their back and feet, being unable to walk far sometimes, legs buckling underneath them, and so forth. I had all those issues.

Weeks later I went into hospital to have different type of test. Evidently the doctor thought I may have a clot on my lungs. With my medical notes on my lap, I was left alone in the ward by the nurse, so I decided to sneak a look through my notes. The result of my CT scan stated in bold letters that I had Arachnoiditis. My initial reaction was one of shock and I re-read the sentence three times. I took out the CT scan report from my medical records for proof as I was well aware that Arachnoiditis was a taboo subject, covered up by medics because, in part, human error was to blame for the condition. Instead of it being flushed out after the examination, the oil-based dye was leaving droplets in the spine, causing serious side effects. I started to ask my consultant questions, who denied that I had the incurable condition. But I knew differently and I was furious. I racked my brain to think of a way to get my case noticed.

During all this our second son Ryan, was born and we decided to sell Sharon's flat in Roehampton and move to the Isle of Wight in 1993. I missed the place. Although I couldn't work I was determined to find out more about Arachnoiditis, so I contacted the Self Help Group, which had been formed a few years earlier. I returned to British Rail and they put me in a booking office on the Island, but within a few weeks I was off sick again. This is when it was decided by BR doctors that I should be medically retired, due to Arachnoiditis. Sharon wasn't happy that I couldn't work any more and didn't offer me much encouragement when I said I had joined a support group.

"I dunno know why you can't just keep out of it, Ron. Get on with your life for God's sake!" she exclaimed.

"I want to warn people about this problem," I reminded her.

"Don't ask me to get involved. I've got enough to do," she snapped.

I didn't expect any backing. It was my problem and my fight. With the Self Help Group behind me I intended to warn others of the dangers of this crippling disease. I heard that The Self Help Group was looking for a new Chairman as the previous one was too ill to continue. I decided to put myself forward to be Chairman, in order to carry on the battle to get things changed. I was angry that doctors were playing with our lives, telling us our pain was in our heads. The drug companies were making millions from the use of these dyes and never put any warnings on the packaging. The group and I dreaded another Thalidomide situation. What we wanted was the truth so I started a campaign with Isle of Wight Radio and the local newspaper, 'Isle of Wight County Press'. I wrote to the Department of Health demanding to know why, as patients, we weren't warned of the risks involved through informed consent. The government tried to sweep the matter under the carpet by stating that it was up to each individual doctor to take the responsibility to inform patients of any side effects and risks.

The news about my campaign was spreading fast. 'Meridian TV' and 'BBC South Today' were on my doorstep wanting the story and I also contacted my local hospital St Mary's and spoke with Dr. Ian Moyle, the Medical Director and Consultant in charge of diagnostic imaging. He stated that there was no evidence to back up my claims, as did his counterpart at Southampton General Hospital, where I had my second back surgery in 1984. I also contacted the Royal Society of Radiologists in London. They told me they didn't like doing myelography's and would have preferred to use MRI Scanners, but they were only available in one or two private hospitals across the country as they cost £2,000,000 each. MRI Scanners are non invasive and give more accurate diagnoses. Dyes are not inserted into the spine and the procedure is painless.

In the USA they were more advanced with diagnosing technology and it was through my research that I contacted a Consultant called Dr. Charles Burton MD, an expert on Arachnoiditis, based in America. Dr. Burton confirmed what we in the Self Help group knew all along and suddenly people including doctors and the government were taking note, but this was only after an adjournment debate in the House of Commons from my then MP Barry Field. Meetings with all political parties and myself took place at the Department of Health. At last Arachnoiditis was being recognized and eventually more money became available for MRI Scanners, plus changes in rules on informed consent throughout the NHS were put in place. However, on the Isle of Wight we needed a MRI Scanner badly, as we only had access to a mobile one which was brought across from the mainland once a month and waiting lists were enormous.

So, with the help of the local newspaper, I started a fund raising campaign to buy an MRI scanner for the Island. I held charity shows with the help of local talent and top stars like Lee John, 'Imagination' and 'The Barron Knights' supported the appeal, giving their services free for the cause. The people who lived on the island were also doing charity runs and all sorts of daft things to add to the fund. We needed to raise £1,500,000, and within two years we had the money. Everyone involved in the campaign was wonderful and the scanner is still saving lives.

However, my own back problem wasn't getting any better and I was in constant chronic pain. But then I heard about a new pain management treatment that had just been set up at St. Thomas's Hospital in London, called Input. I made a few enquiries and went for an appointment with a Dr. Pither, the consultant running the programme. With Input I was taught how to control pain, rather than let it control my life. I learnt about stretching exercises, relaxation techniques and meditation. I went there using a walking stick and on painkilling medication and came away without my stick and off painkillers. I felt better than I had for years. Although I still suffer from pain I know how to manage it.

It was great to be able to pick my kids up again. The worst part of any kind of serious pain is that it affects the way you interact with your children. There were times when I felt like a terrible father because I couldn't play with my children properly.

It was the morning of the 16th of February 1993 and my brother-in-law John had come to help me decorate the house. I waved the boys off to school and I was stripping the wallpaper in the living room when suddenly I felt giddy and had to hold on to the wall to steady myself.

"John, I feel funny. I'm going for a lie down upstairs," I said.

"You OK?" he asked, pulling strips of paper off the wall.

"Yeah, I'll be fine."

When I got upstairs and lay on the bed I felt a searing pain creeping down my left arm and I was weak and unable to do anything, even sit up. Terrified, I called down to John, who took one look at me and ran back downstairs to call my doctor.

"You take it easy, Ron. The doc's on his way." He was standing above the bed with a worried look on his face.

"I feel dozy, John," I said.

"Nothing new there then, eh?" John laughed.

It was only a matter of 10 minutes until the doctor arrived, but it seemed like hours to me. The pain in my arm had got much worse and I was sweating heavily. The doctor gave me an injection for the pain and an aspirin, and announced that he was calling an ambulance, to take me to hospital. Although I was frightened and didn't know what was happening, the pain from my arm eased as the morphine began to kick in. The ambulance arrived and after being wired up to a monitor I was rushed to hospital with John by my side, looking pale and scared. I was told by medical staff that I was exhibiting classic heart problem symptoms, so I was taken into coronary care and monitored. My sister and Sharon had gone shopping.

The next morning the nurses looked at the monitor and rushed to get the doctor as I was now in the midst of having a full blown heart attack, which was surreal to hear because I felt no discomfort. John and my sister looked horrified while medical staff hurried around me, shouting out instructions to one another. Sharon visited too although she didn't say all that much to me, apart from the fact that it was my own fault for spending too much time and effort on the campaign.

"I've said it before an' I'll say it again – you're mad, you are, Ron," Sharon said, shaking her head.

I was kept in hospital for ten days to recover, during which time a stent was put in one of my arteries. But for the next three years I was living on my nerves, frightened I was going to have another heart attack. When I argued with Sharon it was all I could think about. My confidence really took a dive; if I felt the slightest angina pain I fretted that it was happening again.

But something positive also came out of my experience. It gave me a new attitude and I was keen to make the most of my life. After some serious thought I realized that I wasn't happy in my marriage and hadn't been for a very long time. Sharon and I hardly spoke and we never went anywhere or did anything together. We were only a couple out of habit and I'm sure we weren't ever madly in love, even when we first met. I was living in a bed and breakfast and Sharon had offered me a place to live, that's all it boiled down to I'm ashamed to admit. Back in those days I went through life with my eyes shut and my head down – while I hoped for the best. I can't blame my stupidity on youth as it was a pattern I followed well into later adulthood. But I do think that I was running from something, that I spent most of my life being afraid. Marriage was my comfort blanket.

Over the years Sharon and I had grown apart and already being fed up with all the campaigning, she no doubt felt that my heart attack was the last straw, that it was brought on by the stress of the campaign and it was my fault I was in such a predicament. She had watched me doing so much charitable work and maybe she felt that charity should begin at home and that I was neglecting her. I don't know for sure. But the aftermath of my heart attack and my anxiety issues had brought everything to a head and I realized we couldn't keep the relationship afloat any more. It's hard to make a marriage work when it is filled with so many dramas or when the people in it have no energy left to even hold a decent conversation.

Mind you we did have a good holiday, just a few months after my heart attack. We with my sister Pauline and John went to Cyprus. Ryan, our youngest, he was three years old at the time, had a coke, John had a brandy and coke. Somehow Ryan picked up the wrong drink, in minutes he was wobbling and speaking slurry, he had the brandy and coke, Ryan could not stop giggling, so Sharon picked him up under one arm and marched him off to the apartment for the night to sleep it off. Mind you he had a hangover the next day.

When we returned home, nothing had changed.

Sharon had just come off the phone to her friend when I told "Sharon, I need to discuss something important," I said.

"What?" I could see she was distracted. She didn't like listening to me much in general.

"I want to leave and do this summer season at Bournemouth I'm not happy. I don't think you are either," I said.

"What d'you mean – you want to leave? How long for?" Sharon frowned at me.

"I don't know," I replied.

"If you go, don't come back." Sharon got up and walked out of the room. And that's exactly what I did – I left and didn't return. When Sharon and I divorced in early 1999 we'd been together almost

14 years and the boys were 13 and 11. This time I didn't fall to pieces or punish myself for being a failure. I felt guilt over leaving my children; I loved Denis and Ryan with all my heart but their mother and I had been married long enough to know that we weren't meant to be. I left that house with an overwhelming sense of relief more than anything else.

The council gave me a two-bedroom flat in Ventnor and luckily I had no problems with Sharon as far as the boys were concerned. I saw them about twice a week and often met them outside their school. We'd have a fish and chip supper.

"Are you coming back to live with us and Mum soon?" Ryan asked me a few months after I moved out.

"No, son," I said and smiled sadly at him. "Sorry, but I'm not coming back."

21

I began to take an interest in show business again and was keen to help a young singer called Sam Wakeman. I spotted the 17-year-old in a local talent contest and thought she had an amazing voice. She won the competition and afterwards I went up to her and offered to help her get on in the industry. Firstly, I contacted a friend of mine Bill Padley, a leading songwriter/producer and he gave her some songs he had written and took her into his studio at his home. With Bill's songs I knew she would be on her way. Bill is even more famous today, with hits under his belt for Blue, Atomic Kitten and many others.

I called theatrical agent Johnny Mans and introduced him to Sam, who was immediately booked by Johnny for Norman Wisdom's last UK tour, in 1997. Johnny then asked me if I'd like to be tour manager. I couldn't believe my ears, or my luck. I had always been a big fan and coincidentally it was while I was doing an impression of Norman that I had fallen off stage and hurt my back, making my earlier injury flare up again. I'd already met Tommy Steele, my childhood idol, and now I was going to work with Norman Wisdom I thought that all my birthdays had come at once.

The tour was for a month and was booked into theatres the length and breadth of the country, in places like Southend-on-Sea, Bradford and Norwich. I was shocked to see how fit and energetic Norman was for an 82-year-old, running up and down stairs and going for long jogs in the early mornings, before everyone was awake. It must have been all the fish, chips and mushy peas he ate.

"It's good for ya, Ron! Puts hairs on me chest, dunnit?!" He said to me during a break in between shows. Most of his peas were flicked at me or one of the nearby diners in cafes and restaurants. He was always messing about.

We visited the Motor Show in Birmingham during a break in between performances and Norman climbed under the barrier and on to a revolving platform with a gleaming car on it, to get a closer look. He opened the door and sat in the driver's seat, pretending to drive, and yelled out of the open window in his daft voice, "Oi, oi! Road hog, get out of me way!"

A security guard came bounding over and was obviously horrified to see this little bloke peeping through the windscreen. He was about to get angry when he realised it was Norman and kindly asked him to step down. Norman obliged, but was soon looking around to see what else he could get up to. He was like an excitable kid.

It was getting late into the afternoon and one of the crew went up to Norman and told him we were all hungry.

"Leave it to me," he replied.

He ushered us towards the Bentley stand and was looking at the car on the platform when he was suddenly completely surrounded by salesmen.

"Cor, lovely model, innit?" We could hear Norman saying to the men, nodding and running a hand down the sleek bodywork. "How much d'you say it was again?"

Norman and the rest of us were invited into the VIP area where we were fed canapés and strawberries and cream, washed down with champagne.

"Good 'ere, innit?" said Norman, grinning at us, chomping on a shrimp canape. He had no interest in the cars; he just wanted to get us all fed and watered. He pulled the same stunt at the Jaguar, Rolls

Royce and Mercedes stands. That night we all went home completely full and a little tipsy.

Norman had just had his autobiography released and we were in Ipswich at a book signing when an elderly couple approached him with a copy of his book for him to put his signature on. They both looked dazed, being in the presence of their hero.

"'ello, who should I address this to?" asked Norman, smiling at the couple.

"Mr and Mrs Grimsdale," said the woman.

Norman almost fell off his chair. "Cor, really?! You're really called *Grimsdale*?!"

The couple nodded.

Norman signed the book and kept repeating how pleased he was to meet some real Grimsdales. He told the couple that they had made his day. They went off with big smiles on their faces.

It was the last night of the tour and we were in a theatre in Sevenoaks, Kent. I was in the wings, calling his lighting cues to the technicians, and it was also my job to tell the crew to drop the curtains at the end of the show. But this time Norman didn't step back as quickly as he normally did and my cue was too early. The huge, heavy curtains came hurtling down at 30mph, missing his head by an inch, as he ducked out of the way in the nick of time. I was mortified and ran up to him after the show.

"Cor, that was a close one," Norman said as he came off stage, wearing his famous scruffy gump suit that didn't fit him properly and a lopsided cap.

"Sorry, Norman. I could've killed you! You OK?" I said.

He was laughing and he slapped me on the arm and winked: "You after my act, Ron?"

Although Norman's set ran for over an hour each time he always insisted on meeting his fans after the show backstage, signing every autograph until they were all gone. Each show was a sell-out. It was a good start for Sam as well. The experience she had with the tour had afforded her the opportunity to further her career. That Christmas Sam and I were invited to St James's Palace to the Lest We Forget Association's annual Christmas dinner, with the Duchess of Kent, which was a great honour. Sam performed along with Paul Daniels and many other household names, but soon after she decided to get married and live in America.

I don't remember the exact date simply because the news sent my mind into such a spin and I can hardly recollect the full conversation but it was inching towards the latter part of the 90s when I heard something startling. I was visiting my parents and we were all in the kitchen, having a fairly innocuous conversation when Mum suddenly changed the subject.

"Did you hear about Frank Bush, Ron?"

"What?" Hearing that name made my heart race and I felt my hands shake. I gripped the edge of the dinner table and sat down.

"You alright?" asked Dad.

"Yeah…" Although I often thought about what Frank done to me, I hadn't heard his name spoken out loud in a long time. "Can I have a glass of water, Dad?"

Dad filled a tumbler from the tap and passed it to me.

"You sure you're alright?" he said.

"Yeah, think I might be getting a cold," I replied, trying to ignore the mounting panic.

"Shame isn't it, Ron?" said Mum.

"What is?" I asked.

"Frank's dead."

Mum carried on speaking; no doubt filling me in on the details surrounding Frank's death, but all I could hear was the blood pounding in my ears and I felt hot and dizzy. I could see Frank's sweating face looming above me and feel his fat hands on my bare skin. Waves of nausea flooded through my body and I was dying to run out of the room, but I couldn't because my parents would ask questions. So I sat there, hoping I appeared normal to them.

My dad was telling me that they had read about Frank's funeral in the local newspaper and I recall thinking that he didn't deserve a proper burial; that he was an evil pervert and I wished that my parents could know the truth about him. I was almost 50 then but when I heard that news it took me straight back to the times Frank Bush molested me in his house when I was a little boy.

I still regretted the fact that I hadn't had the courage to report him to the police and I felt fresh shame at my lack of guts wash over me. God only knows how many other children he might have targeted. I took responsibility for that. There was a small consolation to be taken from this recent change in circumstance though; Frank's death meant that he couldn't do any more harm. I believed in God and was never a vengeful man but I had no forgiveness in my heart for Frank. I don't now.

"Shame don't you think, Ron?" sighed Mum. "He was such a nice man."

I nodded: "Yes, such a shame, Mum."

After the Norman Wisdom tour I decided to visit my eldest daughter, Suzanne, then 31, and her husband and my grand children in Australia as I hadn't seen them for seven years. Suzanne and her husband Ian moved out there in 1996 but she separated from him within six months. They had two children together, Simon and Charlene, but when she met her new fella he took her children on as his own and they went on to have another two together.

Although my children from my first marriage had been kept away from me while they were young, when they got older and more independent Suzanne and Michael had called me and we often met up and kept in touch by phone. Lorraine was annoyed with me. I was sad that I had missed out on such a chunk of their childhoods but I told myself that there was no room for bitterness. The past had been very difficult but all three of them had turned out well and I built up a strong relationship with Suzanne and Michael as time passed. I introduced Michael to some people in London and lined him up with a job in a friend's recording studio when he was 23. Michael did very well for himself in the music business and he eventually moved to Italy to set up his own studio. I didn't get to see him as often as I would have liked but we spoke on the phone, when we could. I clung on to the hope that Lorraine would change her mind about seeing me. She was angry about all my marriages, who could blame her.

I booked my flight to Oz via Singapore, where I stayed over for a few days and happened to get chatting to a guy also staying in the same hotel called Kenny, a 22 year old Singaporean who had his own recording studio called Tiny Box Music. We hit it off straight away and Kenny gave me his card and promised to keep in touch. It was the first time I had been to the country and I loved the place at once, noticing how friendly the local people were.

I was skint, as usual, so my credit card took a quite a bashing throughout this trip, where I stayed in a rather plush hotel, with marble floors and vases of flowers everywhere.

The first night there I spotted a woman with big brown eyes and short black hair sitting with a group of women in the hotel bar. I was on my own, reading the paper, but as soon as I saw what a lovely smile the woman had my interest in 'The News of the World' fizzled out. I tried to catch her eye but she was laughing with her friends and her attention wasn't focussed in my direction. Eventually I plucked up the courage to wander past her a few times, pretending I was on my way to the gents, hoping she would notice me. On my third attempt she did. She turned her head and smiled at me.

"Hello there," I said, throwing her a cheeky wink. "Are you from these parts?"

"Sorry?" She shook her head. Her first language obviously wasn't English.

"Do you live here?" I asked. She looked like a local to me.

"In the hotel?" the woman laughed, as did her friends, who I noticed were also elbowing one another.

"No, round 'ere," I explained, feeling a bit of a lemon.

"I live near, yes. You live here?" the woman said.

"No, I live in England. I'm Ron."

"Your name?" she asked.

"Yes."

"I'm Aisha."

"Nice. Can I get you ladies a drink?" I said. Her friends gave me their drink orders.

"A coke please," replied Aisha.

"You don't want me to stick a stiff one in it?" I asked.

Her face was blank.

"Vodka? Brandy?"

"No, I don't drink alcohol."

"Oh," I said. "That's good."

"Coke's fine." She gave me a lovely big smile and I thought: *way-hey, looks like I'm in!*

We spent all evening chatting about our lives and families (I didn't mention my wedding habit though) and Aisha told me that she was half Indian and half Malaysian. She offered to show me around Singapore as it was her day off the next day. She took me around the sights like Boat Quay and Tanjong Pagar and later I flew on to Australia to see my daughter and grandkids for a fortnight.

On my return to the UK I stopped over again in Singapore and met up with Aisha. We had a great time and I was sad to return home. I visited several times in the following months and in between sightseeing and eating out Aisha and I stayed in different hotels, making love. When I asked her if we could go to her place she told

218

me that she still lived at home with her parents and that they wouldn't like it if she brought a man back. As she was 40 years old I found it strange that she wasn't allowed to introduce boyfriends to her family but I let the subject drop. I was in Singapore and I knew the culture was different to the UK. I found Aisha exciting and exotic, mainly because I'd met my other women in bingo halls and holiday camps.

We were getting dressed and were about to leave our hotel room when Aisha looked at me seriously. She had finished doing up her cream blouse and was putting on lip gloss.

"What is it?" I asked.

"I think you should know I'm Muslim, Ron."

"That's nice," I said, pulling up my briefs.

"You don't understand." Aisha shook her head.

"Sure, I know about Muslims," I shrugged. "You don't eat bacon and…"

"No, I mean that now I have slept with you we have to get married. I have shamed my family," she sniffed and tears filled her eyes.

I felt my face flush and my heart race. I opened my mouth to say something but couldn't force the words out. I didn't want to get married again and I'd only known her a few months. I felt that it was rushing things, but Aisha kept repeating that she had committed a sin in the eyes of Islam and that her family would be outraged if they found out we had had sex. She became hysterical and I was worried the people in the next room might think I was beating her up.

"They will disown me! I'll be hated by the neighbours!" she cried. I couldn't understand why her neighbours had anything to do with our business.

"We don't have to tell them," I reasoned. "I don't tell my neighbours anything. In fact, I hardly know them, apart from Mrs. Smith at number 22."

"It's wrong, Ron! You don't understand my culture. I'll be hated by my family and the community!"

She looked like she was going to have a nervous breakdown and I felt responsible, even though I hadn't realised that she was Muslim and therefore the significance of her beliefs. I was trapped but I had to do the decent thing. I had always considered myself a gentleman.

I patted her arm. "OK, don't get upset, love. Let's get married - if it'll help."

Aisha smiled and wiped her nose on a tissue. "Can I come to England afterwards?"

"Isle of Wight," I corrected her.

"Isle of Wight," she repeated.

"Of course. You'll love it!"

Aisha wrapped her arms around my neck and kissed me on the cheek. "Oh, thank you, Ron!"

"You're welcome," I said.

22

Before Aisha and I could marry I had to convert to Islam otherwise we wouldn't have been allowed to wed. I was accepted into the Muslim community and given the name Rondel Mohammed Abdullah which I wasn't keen on but Aisha and her mother had picked it for me so I didn't like to moan.

We were in a hotel bar, where we often met, and were talking about the wedding when Aisha said that her mum had been asking personal questions about me.

"What is it?" I asked.

"Mother wanted to know if you've been circumcised."

"I think you might have noticed by now that I'm not," I pointed out.

"I told Mum that you are but it's a lie so I thought that maybe…"

I held my hand up, cutting her off. "No way am I getting the snip!" I cupped my hand over my privates, wincing.

"But, Ron… it's important to my family…"

"Not as important as my family jewels are to me," I said. "Your mother needn't know the truth."

"But all Muslim men are circumcised…"

"No way, Jose. My willy is my business. And that's final," I said.

"OK," she agreed.

In May 2000 we married in Singapore in a Muslim registry office surrounded by her family. Aisha wore the most amazing Malay gown in gold and I had to wear traditional outfit in the same colour and carry a dagger. I wasn't sure what I was meant to do with it so I waved it about in the air, until Aisha told me to put it in the holster that was attached to the outfit.

Her brother and cousin were witnesses as we were married by the registrar, whose English was very broken and I couldn't understand him most of the time, so I had to ask him to repeat everything slowly for me. Afterwards it was time to go outside in the scorching heat and have the wedding photographs done. My costume and matching headgear was heavy and the sweat rolled down my face while we all posed as hundreds of pictures were taken. I nearly fainted from standing in the sun for so long. When I saw the photos later I looked a terrible sight. My face was burnt bright pink and my high headdress drooped sideways.

When the ceremony was over Aisha's family smiled and chatted away at the wedding breakfast at the Excelsior Hotel – the exact same place we had met up many times for sex - but they were speaking Malay so I had no idea what they were saying. I remember looking around the room at all these strangers in loud colourful gear and thinking, *what have I done?* I didn't love Aisha. She was a cracking girl and I fancied her, but that was about it. I'd just come out of a 14-year marriage and was feeling vulnerable. You would assume that I'd have learned my lesson but it seemed that I was building up quite an impressive habit.

I watched as Aisha laughed with her family over on the other side of the room. She hardly spoke to me all day, so I sat and twiddled my thumbs until the celebrations were over and it was time to go back to the Isle of Wight. I pushed any worries to the back of my mind and got on with it. I had another wife to think of now.

I got Aisha a visa to live in the UK as my wife, where she worked as a chamber maid in a hotel near where we lived in Ventnor. She saved most of her wages to send back to her family in Singapore who were poor and refused to give me any towards the housekeeping or bills, but she was happy to do most of the cleaning as she was quite traditional in that way. I hardly saw her because she preferred to spend as much time as she possibly could visiting her family and when she was at home with me she would constantly talk about how much she missed home. I was beginning to suspect that she had only married me for a UK visa. Although I found Aisha's lack of interest in me and my own family galling, I wasn't exactly surprised that less than six months after we wed we were hardly sleeping together and only spoke when we had to. We were like strangers sharing a flat.

Apart from seeing Denis and Ryan regularly, I was also in contact with Kelly, my daughter with Kathy, who was 18 and came to visit when she could. Aisha wasn't happy about having any of my kids to stay over and would make herself scarce or hardly say a word when they were around. Pauline and John had moved over to the Isle of Wight too and Aisha wasn't keen to get to spend time with them either.

"Why aren't you interested in getting to know my family?" I asked her once. My sister and brother-in-law had been to visit and Aisha had made an excuse and hidden in the bedroom.

She shrugged. "They aren't *my* family – they're yours," she sniffed as she got ready for bed. "They have come to see you, not me."

I was tempted to tell her that she was selfish but I couldn't be bothered with her attitude. I was just pleased that I had my sister nearby and I was spending time with my children. In fact, the only two I wasn't in contact with was Lee and Craig, from my marriage to Lesley, who had always made it plain that I was to stay well away from her and her dad. I hoped that the opportunity to see the boys would arise somehow. They were both in their 20s and free to do what they wanted. I reminded myself that it was only a matter of time.

While I was happy that I had my most of my family back some sad news soon shook me out of my positive mood. It was early September 2000 when I got a call from my sister telling me that Dad was in Kingston hospital with a chest infection, so we rushed over to the UK as soon as we could. Dad had suffered with chest problems since he had been discharged from the Navy after the war for ill health. But within days he was in a serious condition because he contracted MRSA which weakened his immune system and made his condition much worse.

When my sister, John and I first saw him in the hospital we were shocked to see how ill Dad looked – so thin and pale against the starched white sheets. I was even more angry about the MRSA when the doctors told me that because he was so ill there was no way Dad could go home and be looked after by my mother, who was 81. She was in a terrible state and kept saying that she wanted him with her and I had to tell her that it wasn't possible. I complained to the hospital management about my father's condition but it was too late. The MRSA meant that there was little hope for Dad. We were all too upset to think about legal action.

After a month in Kingston Hospital it was decided that Dad would have to go into a Royal British Legion nursing home, who could give someone like him specialist care day and night. I knew Dad wouldn't want to be away from Mum but he was in no condition to kick up a fuss. I'm not sure that he even knew what was going on around him all the time anyway. He was hooked up to a drip and receiving numerous injections and was asleep a lot. Pauline and I tried to put on a brave front for Mum but we were devastated.

I stayed some of the time with Mum but was generally travelling back and forth between the island and the hospital when I received a call from one of the nurses at The Star and Garter nursing home in Richmond, Surrey. It was 7.30am on October 7th 2000 and the nurse said that my dad had got worse during the night and they didn't expect him to live till the end of the day.

I called Pauline and my dad's sister who lived round the corner from my mum, asking her to go around to Mum's flat and tell her. Pauline, John and I were about to travel to Richmond from Ventnor to be with Dad when at 8.05am I got another phone call from the nursing home to tell me that he had died. He was 85. I was so shocked that I stood there, not knowing what to do. I then had to break the news to my mum on the phone, who cried her eyes out. He was the only man she had ever loved. It broke my heart.

I couldn't believe my lovely Dad was gone. Although he never showed much affection, Pauline and I didn't once doubt that he loved us both. He was just born into a generation that didn't talk about their feelings.

Dad was given a veteran's send-off at Kingston Crematorium on the 16th October that year. Pauline and I decided that Mum shouldn't be on her own so we sorted out a transfer with her housing association and brought her back to the Isle of Wight, where she lived in a flat in the same block as me. I was relieved that Mum was in a place where I could look out for her.

However, my wife was less than impressed with the latest family set up and the atmosphere at home became unbearable when Aisha accused my mother of spying on her. Mum liked to while away her days looking out of her window, which Aisha had to walk past to get to work. My mother would smile and wave at her each morning, as she did when other people passed by her flat.

"Don't be so bloody silly, Aisha," I snapped. "Mum just likes to look out the window! She's got little else to do!"

Mum had recently lost her husband of 61 years and I was disgusted by Aisha's attitude. I had a hunch that divorce number six was on the horizon.

23

I was gutted over the loss of my father and I asked Aisha if she would come to Australia with me to visit my eldest daughter and grandchildren. She refused, saying that she wanted to visit her family in Singapore. So my sister, John and I decided that we would go to Singapore for a break with her. At the end of the week's visit Aisha said she hated the cold of the Isle of Wight and that she was determined to remain in Singapore with her mother for the time being.

Thinking that Aisha might prefer somewhere else I suggested a holiday in Thailand, where I had a friend, who was over there for work. I met Kenny in a Singapore hotel in 1999 and we had kept in touch. He had a lot of business meetings in Thailand and Asia and sometimes asked me along with him, to help look out for potential new singing stars. Kenny was married to his job when I first met him and built up a formidable business reputation, becoming A&R director for Universal Music, Asia.

Again my card took a bashing, plus I had a Singapore Airlines Gold Krisflyer card, where I had enough points for free flights from Singapore to Thailand. I didn't care about the money; I needed a break. I missed Dad and wanted my wife to share a relaxing holiday with me.

But Aisha said that she wouldn't leave her mother and it finally sunk in that I had been used. I'd been stupid to marry her in the first place.

My sister and brother in law went home and I flew on to Thailand for four days. It was my first night there when I met a Thai girl called Nus in a restaurant. She offered to show me around town and I took her up on her hospitality. I think I knew what was going to happen. We ended up in bed in a hotel room and had three fun days together – mostly spent having sex if I'm honest about it. When I returned to Singapore I told Aisha about the affair straight away. She didn't seem upset but said that I was to remain faithful in the future as she was a good Muslim and it was wrong to see other people. By now, I wanted out of the marriage and told her that I couldn't promise that I wouldn't see Nus again, which was a lie. Nus was merely a holiday fling. After less than three years of marriage Aisha and I agreed to divorce and we contacted a solicitor in Singapore. I returned to the Isle of Wight a single man.

I wasn't bitter about the break up but I was in my mid fifties now and realised that I couldn't carry on going from one disastrous marriage to another. It wasn't making me happy and I had felt lonelier being married to Aisha than I did when I was a free agent. It was the first time I really sat down and thought about how foolish I could be sometimes.

Why do I keep doing these things, I asked myself one night just after the divorce was granted. I was sitting in my living room wondering what I was going to do with myself, now I was single once more. It was April 2003 and I decided that I would concentrate on being a good son and dad and not dabble with women again – or not for at least a few years. It was time to break my wedding habit and turn over a new leaf.

In May 2003 I went back to Thailand for a week, where I was introduced to an attractive Thai girl by Kenny in a Bangkok office where he had a meeting with music executives and she was doing secretarial work. She was slim and had long jet black hair. I thought she was pretty.

"Me – Bongkok," she smiled over her desk and then said something else which I couldn't understand. She spoke little English.

I looked at Kenny. "Huh? Her name's Bangkok?"

"No *Bong*kok," he replied.

"No Wan! Wan!" she said loudly, slapping her chest. "I Wan!"

"What does she want?" I asked Kenny, who was laughing.

"No, her nickname is Wan. She prefers it to Bongkok," he explained.

"Can't say that I blame her," I said to Kenny and then smiled at Wan. "I'm Ron."

"Ron." she repeated and grinned.

"Thanks," I smiled back.

Kenny and I arranged to see her a few hours later. That evening she tottered into my hotel bar in a short skirt and stiletto heels with her friend Trish, another local girl, behind her. Kenny interpreted for us.

I found out Wan was 32 and lived nearby. Her mum and dad had died when she was 10 and she brought up her younger sister Nong with the help of her aunt who became their foster mum. Wan was sent to work very young, to help them to survive, which many children in Thailand had to do.

I felt sorry for Wan but told myself not to get too involved, especially after what had happened with Aisha. She seemed keen to get to know me though and we arranged to meet alone the following day. Over the following week I managed to understand her Pidgin English a little better and we went out on the town quite a few times, where she showed me around the local hotspots and bars.

I felt sorry for her because she was living with her aunt and sister in a tiny shack on the river, where they shared the same bedroom. So, I decided to rent a condominium for Wan and her sister, to help get them out of the situation they were in. I was hardly rich myself so yet again my credit card came in handy. My debts were mounting but I pushed any concerns to the back of my mind. I liked Wan and I wanted to help her.

It was a spacious apartment, with two bedrooms, a large kitchen, a good size lounge and a balcony. But it wasn't long before I realised that my new girlfriend was a bit eccentric.

We were eating dinner at the kitchen table when I made a comment about the rice being cold. It wasn't intended to be rude; all I meant was that I was going to heat it up so it tasted nicer. Wan's face changed and she stood and began shouting at me in her own language. I put my hands on her shoulders, trying to get her to sit.

"Wan, calm down," I said.

She was wailing: "You no like my cook!"

I sat and spooned a portion of food into my mouth. "Mmm, lovely. Yum yum!" I said encouragingly.

"You lie!" Wan threw her plate of food against the wall, where globules of rice slid to the floor.

"I'm sorry, Wan," I gabbled, shocked at her outburst. "Please, sit down. It's OK."

"No, I kill myself!" Wan stomped over towards the balcony.

Petrified, I sprinted after her. "Don't be so stupid, Wan!"

"I no stupid! I kill myself!" She flung her leg over the top wooden railing of the balcony and tried to heave herself over the edge. I grabbed the hem of her short skirt and pulled her backwards.

"Wan!" I yelled. "Stop! Please!"

"I jumping!" She again threw both arms over the top rung of the railing and heaved forwards with all her strength.

Realising she was stronger than she looked I was worried. "Help! Help! My girlfriend's trying to kill herself!" I shouted into the night. We were on the sixth floor so God knows who was going to hear me and come running.

"Ron! You love me?" Wan cried, still struggling to launch herself over the balcony.

I levered a foot against the wall at the aide of the balcony, grabbed a handful of the material of the back of her t-shirt and heaved her backwards as I yelled: "Yes, Wan, I love you! OK?"

"OK!" Wan shouted and fell in a heap on top of me and was immediately calm again. She stood and pulled me to my feet.

"OK, we finish eat," she smiled.

I didn't have much of an appetite, but scared of what she might do next, I cleaned my plate.

We'd been an item for a fortnight when I had to return to the UK but the night before Wan seemed different to her usual self. We were cuddled up on the sofa in the living room. Her sister Nong was out at work.

"You're quiet," I said. "What you thinking about?"

"We get married," she blurted and looked at me for a reaction. I felt sick to my stomach.

"It's too soon, Wan," I said quickly.

She shot me an angry look and sat up straight, flinging her arms in the air. "But me love you! Why no marry me?! I ugly? What wrong wiv me?"

I didn't love Wan. I liked her; she was funny, but I found her unsettling.

"Nothing's wrong with you. Let's wait a while. We'll discuss it when I come back next month," I reassured her. I secretly hoped that she'd forget the subject of weddings by the time I returned to Thailand.

Wan was pouting. "OK, we talking when you back."

I kissed her on the cheek. "Good. That's sensible." The relief surged through me.

During the three weeks I was back on the Isle of Wight I spoke to Wan on the phone every night and she seemed upbeat when she spoke of her job and her sister Nong. It wasn't until I set foot back in Bangkok that I found out that Wan had been making a number of plans while I was away.

"What?!" I shrieked. I had literally just plonked my suitcase in the middle of the condominium floor when Wan snaked her arms around my neck and informed me of our upcoming nuptials in a few day's time.

"What wrong, Ron?" She was pouting at me.

I pulled her arms from around my neck. "I told you I didn't want to get married!"

"I finking you like!" Wan wailed.

"I don't like!" I said.

Wan began to cry. "You don't love me! You no wanting me!"

"I do want you, Wan. I don't want to get married though, that's all," I tried to reason with her.

Now she was wailing loudly. "I tell my family! Friends they come. I tell all people we marry!"

"You mean you've sent invites out already?!" I shrieked, slapping my forehead with my hand.

"Yes, they happy!" Wan threw herself on the sofa and sobbed, all the while jabbering on in her own language.

When I got the whole story out of her it transpired that she had booked the register office, had sent invites to over 150 people, had arranged a session with a portrait photographer in his studio prior to the wedding, a Thai tradition, and had bought a wedding dress for her and hired a suit for me. She had also arranged two reception dos on two consecutive nights. The Friday night was for her family and friends and the Saturday was for her old workmates, from a company she used to work for.

I sat on the sofa with my head in my hands and I very nearly cried, too. I was dumbstruck, especially when she handed me the huge bill of accumulated wedding costs which I was expected to pay.

Wan clambered behind me on the sofa and slid a leg either side of my thighs and began to massage the back of my neck.

"We marry, yes?" she said, peering around at me hopefully. "You finking good idea?"

I was determined to get myself out of the situation.

"Yes, Wan…" I lied.

24

Wan had gone to a lot of trouble and she had already tried to throw herself off the balcony once. I knew that she had attempted suicide when a previous boyfriend finished with her so I was worried that she would top herself if I refused to go through with the wedding. Wan became wife number seven. Again, I was the groom at an unusual ceremony, wearing traditional clothing, surrounded by smiling strangers as they celebrated the nuptials. The actual day and two reception parties passed in a blur. I have never been a big drinker but I downed a few brandies in order to numb the worry. Wan was in her element, flitting about laughing with her friends and family. I stood in the background, making small talk and smiling. In my head I was wondering why I was such an idiot. But eventually I got used to the idea that I had another wife, however it struck me pretty much straight away that Wan might well have done it to get herself a UK visa, as she was granted one within days and we were on a plane to the UK weeks after the wedding.

"I excited!" She announced as the plane touched down at Heathrow. "Where sun?" Wan poked her finger towards the sky.

It was a drizzly day in late August and I had already warned Wan about the temperamental UK weather and to buy some warm clothes but she was in a thin pink t-shirt, short skirt and bare legs. When she got off the flight she grabbed me and wailed: "Ooh, I want go home! I cold!"

"Wait till you get on the ferry to the Isle of Wight," I muttered, wondering what my mum was going to make of my new wife and feeling sick at the thought of bringing yet another woman to meet her.

"It hot there?" asked Wan hopefully.

"Nope, 'fraid not," I answered. I explained that although it was summer that in the UK we often had rain.

"I no like," Wan sniffed. "It no good."

"Well there's not much I can do about it," I said. "C'mon, let's go home."

A few days after we had settled in at my Ventnor flat I took Wan around to Mum's place, which was in the same block as mine. I felt particularly nervous because Wan was dressed in a skin tight canary yellow cat-suit and six inch gold sandals with big diamante stones on. The brightly coloured bangles on her wrists make clanking sounds when she moved and her thick pink lip-gloss shone in the morning sunlight. The Isle of Wight locals weren't used to such sights and my mother was usually in a nice floral dress and cardigan. Mum's eyes nearly popped out when she first saw Wan. I stood sheepishly in my mother's living room as Wan rushed over to her in her favourite chair by the window.

"Hi Ron Mummy!" shrieked Wan, hugging Mum and planting lipstick kisses on her cheeks. "I Ron wife!"

Mum's face was blank and she looked up at me warily. "Ron?"

"Mum, remember I told you that I got married in Thailand?"

"Yes, yes, I do," sighed Mum, her hair kept in place by a hairnet.

"Well, this is Wan – my wife…" I pointed at Wan, who went to hug my mother again and was grinning widely.

"Hello," said Mum to Wan. "How are you?"

"I… erm… 32," replied Wan, her hands on her hips.

"No Wan," I said, touching her arm. "Mum asked how you are" Wan was frowning at me.

"Your health…" I carried on.

She was still frowning.

"In England we ask if people are OK when we first meet them…" I said.

She smiled at Mum. "Oh… I good," said Wan, nodding briskly. "Fanks."

"Would you like something to drink?" asked Mum.

Wan's forehead furrowed.

"Want a cup of tea?" said Mum.

"Ah! I go on plane," Wan nodded. There was quiet and Mum looked at me. I shrugged.

"You went where on plane?" Mum asked.

"Toilet," said Wan. I was used to her getting her English mixed up all the time, but I could see that Mum was shocked. Wan was okay when it came to communicating with me but with new people she found it hard. I had spent many hours trying to teach her English but it was like training a cat to fly. She had very little concentration at the best of times.

The three of us smiled at one another in awkward silence and Wan walked over and studied the framed pictures of Mum and Dad together on the mantelpiece. She picked one of the photos up and frowned at it.

"Who this funny old man with Mummy?" she suddenly asked me, prodding a long red polished nail on the glass. I sighed and looked over at Mum apologetically. I had told Wan about my dad but she often didn't understand me and would nod, giving me the impression that she had digested everything I said. When I glanced over at my mother again her shoulders shook with laughter and she was covering her mouth with her hand.

"I like this one, Ron," she said, cocking her head at my new wife.

Wan and I hadn't been in the Isle of Wight long when I found out that she had a fair list of hang ups. She didn't like me touching her intimately and our sexual routine consisted of her touching me and then she climbed on top for intercourse. When I suggested that we spice things up she would either shout or cry, so I gave up. I also found out that she was addicted to slimming pills and hardly ate. She was a tiny girl and didn't need dieting supplements but as usual she never listened to sense. However, it wasn't long before she demanded that I pay for plastic surgery for her.

"I don't have that kind of money, Wan," I said. "You don't need it anyway." We were in the living room, watching TV on a Saturday evening. She preferred to stay indoors because of the cold.

"I fat! I ugly!" she wailed.

"You're beautiful," I said, trying to hug her, but she pushed me away and jumped to her feet. She then shot her left hand up in the air and grabbed the flesh of her underarm.

"I want cut it off - here!" she demanded, pointing at the offending area.

"You want plastic surgery on your underarms?" I was dumfounded. Not only was she very thin but I had assumed she would want a boob job or something like that.

"I fat!" she hollered, tears brimming.

"You are not fat, Wan!"

"I is!" She cried, still pointing at the flesh of her underarm. "I big fat ugly lady!"

"Don't be so bloody silly," I laughed. "The only place you need plastic surgery is on your tongue," I joked, trying to lighten the atmosphere.

Wan poked her tongue out and grabbed it, her face worried. "What wrong wiv it?"

"'Cos your English is so bad! Ha ha!" I chuckled.

"I fink you laugh at me!" she wailed loudly.

Wan didn't understand my joke and wouldn't have cared anyhow. She was in one of her deep sulks now, which could last for days – until she got what she wanted. But I had no money for surgery and I kept pointing this out. Eventually she came around but my lack of funds was a big problem for her. She had initially thought that because I was British that I was rich.

We were back in Thailand soon after our arrival in Ventnor and as I still had a few months rent paid on the apartment we stayed there. During a shopping trip in Bangkok Wan found out just how poor I was. We were walking down a busy main street, filled with jewelry stores, when she kept stopping and staring in the shop windows.

"Buy me!" Wan was pointing at a gold necklace with a diamond pendant. She leaned on the window and peered longingly at the item, her cheek pressed on the glass.

I tried to pull her away from the window but she wouldn't move. "I can't afford gold jewellery, Wan!"

"I want!" she cried, stamping her foot on the pavement. "I your wife! You buy gold!"

"I'm not rich. I have no money!" I replied.

"You no good husband!" she yelled, making passers-by stop and stare. I felt my face flush with humiliation.

"Wan, we're in public. Shush," I said.

Wan was crying like a little girl, with tears streaming down her face, making her mascara run in black lines down her cheeks. "You my husband and you no love me!"

"Oh for God's sake, Wan! Be quiet!" I spat.

"You no love me!" She screamed and stamped her foot and then carried on shouting in her own language. A small group of Thai men in suits had stopped walking and were looking at her and laughing.

By this time I'd had enough; I grabbed Wan by the arm and gently propelled her along the street, in the direction of home. As soon as we got into the apartment Wan made a beeline for the balcony and immediately took a running jump towards the wooden railings on the edge, her arms flat out in front of her like Superman.

"I killing myself!" she wailed. I ran after her and grabbed her by her handbag, pulling her backwards. Wan let the bag drop to the floor and made another move to jump over the balcony, hoisting her skirt up around her bottom as she went. She looped a leg over the top of the railing, flashing the gusset of her red knickers.

"Wan!" I shouted and grabbed her around the waist from behind but she wouldn't budge and continued to shriek that she wanted to jump. At my wit's end, I managed to get her to calm down and said that I would ask her friend to talk to her, who lived on the next floor up. She was a Thai girl and would be able to interpret for us. Wan agreed to speak to her friend, who I rushed to find. I told the girl what had happened and that although I was English I wasn't rich and couldn't afford gold. A few hours later the friend left, having talked Wan down from the edge of the balcony. My wife sat on the sofa sulking, with mascara trails still visible down her cheeks. She was sniffing and saying nothing, just staring into the distance. We'd been married two months. I was exhausted and fed up with her tantrums.

"This isn't working. I think we should get divorced," I said.

Wan spun around to look at me and grabbed my arm. "You no divorce! I sorry!"

"I can't make you happy…"

Wan began to wail again. "I love you!"

With our limited communication skills Wan persuaded me to go to a Buddhist temple the next day so I could speak to the head monk. He explained to me that it was part of the Thai culture to provide for the wife and that I should give Wan whatever she asked for. I replied that I was far from rich but again I was told that it was my role to give my new wife jewellery, designer clothes and anything else she wished for. As I looked at the little bald fella in his brown robes I thought: *It may be your culture to do that, mate, but it ain't mine.*

As far as I was concerned I'd provided Wan and her sister with a home and I'd done my best to help her. I wasn't a mug. I already had mountains of debts on my card from the wedding she had arranged behind my back. I was beginning to feel used. How I wished I'd never clapped eyes on her in the first place.

I returned to the UK and Wan stayed in Thailand, during which time she ended up in hospital due to over-use of dieting pills and I had to stick around in Ventnor because my mother was ill with a heart condition. Eventually Wan got better and came over to see Mum, who was fond of my wife. I could see that Wan was amusing and was glad that she lightened Mum's spirits, who was now in her mid 80s.

It was Tuesday 24th February and at 8.30 that morning I got a phone call from my mum.

Her voice was subdued. "Ron, I don't feel well," she said.

"What's wrong?"

"I keep being sick."

"Mum, we'll be round in a minute."

I replaced the receiver and looked at Wan, who was still in her night clothes. "Mum's ill. We have to go and see her."

Wan ran to the bedroom to get changed. Minutes later we let ourselves into Mum's flat with the spare key she had given me. She was sitting in her favourite armchair by the living room window with a grey washing up bowl by her side. Wan and I hurried over to her.

"Mum, you OK?" I whispered.

Her eyes were watery and she was pale.

Wan hugged her. "Mummy, what wrong?"

"I feel funny." My mum's voice was wobbly and her breath made a rattling sound. Wan looked at me with fear in her eyes.

"I'm calling the doctor," I said and ran to the phone. When I explained Mum's state Doctor Mason said that he would be around straight away. His surgery was only five minutes down the road so he was as good as his word.

A little bloke with glasses arrived, holding a black case and he immediately began to fire questions at me. Mum was half asleep in her chair and Wan sat on the arm, stroking Mum's hand, with tears in her eyes.

"I'm calling an ambulance," said Doctor Mason. His voice was calm and professional but I could see the concern in his expression and my stomach began to churn. I was terrified of losing my mother. She was everything to me. I drew closer to her, to tell her that everything was going to be okay when Wan let out a gasp. Mum's breathing began to sound laboured and her eyes rolled upwards.

"Mummy!" Wan screamed and held her.

"Mum, Mum?" I said, leaning over her and taking her hand. "Mum, speak to me!"

The doctor pulled me out of the way gently and all I can recall is the sound of Wan becoming hysterical and the doctor speaking to Mum and taking medical apparatus out of his case. I had no idea what was going on. I prayed that Mum would be alright while I paced up and down on the living room carpet. I then took her hand in mine again.

"Help Mummy! Please! Help Mummy!" Wan shrieked at the doctor. "No let her die!"

"Calm down – please," said Doctor Mason.

Moments later I felt a hand on my arm. "Your mother has had a heart attack, Mr Sheppard. I'm sorry," Dr. Mason said. He was closing his case and looking at me earnestly. "There was nothing that could be done. I'm so sorry."

I squeezed my mother's hand. "Mum?" I said. I felt tears run down my face.

"No!" yelled Wan, her cheeks wet from crying. "Why?" she glared at the doctor. "Why she die?"

"She had a massive heart attack," he said quietly.

"No! Mummy!" Wan cried over and over again, her arms around my mother's neck. In a daze I said goodbye to the doctor and took Wan back to our flat to try and calm her down. I then called my sister and gave her the terrible news. When she turned up with John she was inconsolable and we hugged for a long while.

"I'm so sorry," said John, red-eyed. "She was a lovely lady."

"I know," I sobbed.

It hadn't really hit me properly then. I was in a state of shock. But my mother's death was a huge blow, especially seeing her pass away in front of me like that. I loved her dearly and it was the worst thing that had ever happened to me. A hollow, dark feeling began to settle in.

25

The doctor cancelled the ambulance and called the local undertaker for us. My mum's body was removed from her flat and taken to a chapel of rest. She was cremated and her and my dad's ashes were placed together in a little plot we had bought on Apse Heath, Isle of Wight. It provided great comfort to my sister and me, knowing they were together. After the death of my mum I felt very numb at first and then I began to notice that old sensation of anxiety returning. I was alone and scared.

The day after Mum's funeral Wan flew back home and I followed two weeks later. I was lost I guess and didn't want to be in the Ventnor flat on my own. Most nights were spent in front of the TV, with Wan mimicking the karate kicks in the fight sequences of her favourite movies, her arms and legs going everywhere while she shouted at the TV. I used to watch her open mouthed.

One morning Wan sat me down on the sofa in the living room of our Bangkok apartment.

"Ron, I not happy," She said.

"OK," I agreed.

"I like divorce," she said.

"OK." The relief swept through me.

She peered at me intently. "I have good idea."

"What?"

"You come here, holiday, and we do sex."

"What?" I was shocked.

"We divorce. You come Thailand. You do sex with me."

"No it's OK, Wan. Thanks all the same," I replied.

I was appalled by her suggestion. The sex between us wasn't very good anyhow. And I certainly didn't intend to spend my holidays with my ex wife.

"But…" She looked offended.

I patted Wan's hand. "Thanks for the offer though. Most kind."

"You fink 'bout it," Wan smiled.

We went to the same Bangkok register office we were married in just eight months before and the divorce was finalized by the official who had carried out the wedding ceremony.

"I know you two," the woman smiled as she looked over the paperwork.

I smiled back sheepishly. "Hi," I said.

There was no waiting around for a decree absolute. We simply had to both agree to end the marriage. After we signed the paperwork and the official announced we were divorced Wan and I stepped out into the sunshine.

"OK. I better go back to the hotel now," I said. I was staying at the Asia Hotel in Bangkok.

"OK, you come visit next year." Wan waved and walked away. "I ring you!"

I had married Wan because I felt sorry for her, not because I loved her. I doubted that I would ever see her again. During the flight to the UK the only woman on my mind was my mum.

When I got back to my flat in Ventnor I felt waves of bleakness engulf me. Realizing that I was in trouble I went to my doctor, who told me that my mum's death had triggered depression and anxiety. He prescribed Prozac. I don't recall taking it for a long period of time.

The death of my mother made me focus on the darkness in my past and my waking thoughts and dreams began to concentrate on Frank and the abuse again. Frank Bush was never completely gone

243

from my mind but there were times over the past 48 years when I could go a whole week or fortnight without thinking about him all that much.

The nightmares started again: being chased by dark figures, their hands reaching out for me.

I wanted everyone around me and everything else to go away. I wanted my mum back and my memories of Frank to disappear forever. Not knowing what to do, I picked up the phone and called my friend Kenny in Singapore, who was a great listener. He spoke about God and how he could help me. I had never been overly religious and was doubtful of Kenny's suggestion. I thanked him for his support and said that I would speak to him another time.

That night I slept in my clothes, with the bedside lamp switched on. The panic swelled in my chest and when I eventually dropped off the nightmares began again. When I woke I was drenched in sweat and shaking. Every night was the same and each day I lay on my sofa, avoiding the phone and refusing to turn the radio on any more. The local station had been playing clips about me: "why is Ron Sheppard Britain's most married man?" and "Who thinks Ron Sheppard has an obsession with women?", the list went on. They had found out about my seventh marriage breaking down and were discussing it, asking the public to call in with their views. It was mortifying. I knew the radio presenters personally and felt humiliated and betrayed.

I stopped going out and wouldn't answer the door. I did my best to swallow the ever present panic and tried to block out the black thoughts.

Eventually though I weakened. In my mind I was useless – a useless husband, son, father and person. I had been tainted since childhood and was a failure as an adult in my opinion. My latest marriage was over and both my lovely parents were gone.

What do I have to live for? I asked myself. Frank Bush knew I was bad through and through. He had told me enough times. I sat up, picked up the bottle of Prozac pills from off the coffee table and unscrewed the lid. But as the pills fell into my hand I began to cry. I couldn't do it. Calling myself a coward, I cried myself to sleep, curled into a ball on the sofa.

When I calmed myself down hours later I said to myself that I had to do something or I was going to lose my mind. It was obvious to me that I had been keeping my secret inside me for far too long. My mother's death had changed something in me. Now that she was gone, as was my dad, I had no reason to hide away. Nothing I said or did could hurt them. It was time to speak to someone about what had happened to me as a child. I needed to be free.

With a shaking hand I picked up the phone and dialled Kenny's number in Singapore. There was no way I could tell him about Frank but I knew he was a Christian as he recorded Christian songs at his record company that he owned and he was affiliated with Christian fellowships. I trusted him more than anyone else so I took Kenny's advice and contacted The Christian Fellowship in the Philippines.

Sitting at my old pc in the living room, I spilled out my whole life story in an email to complete strangers. I told them all about Frank, my sins, my previous seven marriages, everything. Within a day I received an email from the fellowship, written by a young lady named Rowena, who told me to call her Weng which was her nickname. She sent me a copy of Psalm 32: *Happy are those whose sins have been forgiven and whose wrongs are pardoned. Happy is the one whom the Lord does not accuse of doing wrong and is free from all deceit.*

These words gave me new hope and started to rebuild my confidence. I began to wonder if Weng was some kind of sign; that my life was going to get better. Weng's mother and brother were pastors in the Philippines and during the next few weeks they were like my adopted family. They didn't judge me; they just read my letters and offered help and guidance over the phone.

I felt that if I confessed my sins God would punish me, but then I re-read the verse from Psalms 32 that Weng had sent me. One evening I knelt down at the coffee table with my hands clasped and my eyes closed and prayed for forgiveness and repented all my sins. The last time I had spoken to the God was with anger a couple of months earlier when my mother died. The bitterness at my loss boiled over and I asked him why he had taken someone so wonderful from me. Now I openly apologised to God for my stern words, with tears running down my face. I asked him for forgiveness and to save me.

Those 15 minutes of prayer brought peace back into my life and I felt lighter than I had in years. My sceptic thoughts continued to surface though. I felt that my past was less than pure and that I had a lot to be forgiven for.

Unable to sleep I telephoned Weng early the next morning in the Philippines. I told her that I had prayed to God and asked for forgiveness. It was 2:00 am over there and I had forgotten that they were eight hours ahead of us in the UK.

"I've just realised what time it is!" I said. "Sorry! I must have woken the whole family!"

"It's OK, Ron. They're all asleep. Don't worry," Weng replied and we chatted for a long while, with Weng telling me a little more about her life in the village of Santa Rosa in the province of Laguna in the Philipines.

Weng explained that she and her parents lived in a two bedroom house which was attached to a church hall and owned by a Korean pastor. They were the caretakers and this helped Weng's mum continue her ministry within the church. Weng never complained about anything but I realised that they lived in poverty from her description of her daily life. It touched me greatly that these people had very little yet they wanted to help a complete stranger. So, I was even more surprised and humbled when I was invited to visit my new friends. I booked a flight straight away.

On Sunday 31st May 2004 I walked out of Manila airport via a subway and I did a double take when I saw hundreds of people behind barriers, waving hands in the air and shouting out in a foreign language. Weng had said that she was going to bring some of her family to meet me and I thought to myself: *surely they aren't all her family!*

It reminded me of the TV footage when the Beatles had been mobbed by fans.

I was apprehensive because I wasn't sure if I was going to recognise Weng as we had only seen a photo of each other. So, I was manically bobbing up and down, trying to see over the tops of people's heads, but there was no sign of Weng.

"Oh dear," I said aloud. "Where are you, Weng?" I felt a pat on the arm. A tiny Filipino lady was at my side. She held up her mobile phone. "Would you like to use this to call your friend?"

"Oh, that's kind. Thank you," I said and tapped in Weng's number into the keypad. After I said hello to Weng her voice seemed to get closer and to my surprise I saw that she was right behind me. I smiled when I saw an attractive woman in her mid 20s with long black hair, wearing a brown top and black trousers.

"All these people, they're not your family, are they?" I blurted out.

Weng laughed and said, "No!" This is where everyone meets family and friends off flights."

While we made our way to the mini bus to take us to their home I met Weng's mum and her three brothers and their wives and children, who had also come to greet me. The temperature on the bus was at least 33 degrees, which had no air conditioning. Drips of sweat trickled down my face within minutes as we swept through little towns towards Santa Rosa. I looked out of the window at the great puffs of dust that billowed up from the tyres of the mini bus which made its way down sun baked roads. I thought how lush and green the UK was in comparison.

Santa Rosa itself was a busy village which was lined with shops that had bars at the windows to deter robbers. The mini bus drew up outside a two storey white concrete house in a side street which was filled with young people roaring about on motorbikes, a common choice of transport in the area.

Weng's family made me very welcome and we sat around talking after a tasty fish and rice dinner. Weng and her mum were the only two who could understand and speak English, so they interpreted for everyone.

When it grew late I was shown to a tiny room with a mattress on the floor. Weng's parents had given up their bed for me and they slept on the ground in the church hall that was adjoined to the house, along with the rest of the family which totalled 14 people, all lying on cardboard. Weng used the only other bedroom that was available as they had South Korean students occupying the upstairs of the house. She slept on cardboard, too.

I couldn't believe my eyes when I saw how this wonderful family lived, as did most other people in the Philippines. It made me realise how lucky I was.

The next morning everyone was up at five am and it was my first chance to wander out into the street with Weng, where we got on a pedicab. I felt bad for the poor fella peddling away on this rusty bike, with us two in this small side car that creaked so much I thought it was about to collapse at any minute.

I was a novelty to the locals because they didn't often they see a westerner in their streets, but they all smiled or waved at me. I watched people walking in between traffic with trays holding cigarettes which they sold to drivers. Although cigarettes were cheap out there, people who smoked could only afford to buy one at a time, not a whole packet. Others were selling bottled water or handmade crafts and many sold goods that they owned or had found, anything to bring in money for food. But everywhere I went I saw that they were happy people, who liked to help one another.

The first Sunday I was there Weng took me to a New Life Pentecostal Church. The Pastor normally presented his service in Tagalog which is the Philippine language, but that day he spoke mainly in English for me, which I thought was incredibly kind. There was a congregation of over 100 and they had a band with singers, guitars, and a keyboard, drums, microphones and full PA. I felt relaxed as we sang gospel songs while people clapped along to the music. It was far different to the traditional services that I had experienced back in the UK when I went to church mainly for weddings or funerals.

Weng and her family were soon told that they would have to find somewhere else to live. The South Korean owner wanted the place vacated in order to rent rooms to visiting students who travelled to the Philippines to learn basic English for a month and have bible study.

I suggested that Weng's mum and dad look for another home which would suit them better. They had done a lot for me and in return I wanted to help them so I said that I would pay the rent and buy furniture for them. So we went to see an agent who showed us around a few properties that were available, including a two-bedroom house in Lahoya, Santa Rosa, which was brand new and only £70 per month. The place was on a site with security guards and a communal swimming pool, surrounded by greenery.

Weng's parents, who were around the same age as me, were very excited on the day they moved in to their new home, along with Weng. Next we had to go and buy furniture and furnishings so my credit card took a little bit of a bashing, but a cooker over there cost just £90, a sofa £70 and beds were around £100. Weng was so happy when we moved the single bed into her room. She walked over and sat down on the squashy mattress placed in the small cream painted room which was to be hers.

She smiled up at me. "My first real bed! Thanks, Ron!"

"No problem," I replied. "It's the least you deserve."

"You're a good friend," Weng said.

"So are you," I nodded.

Weng and her family made me feel like I belonged somewhere. They couldn't do enough for me, from the very first moment I emailed them after I lost my mother. I was so grateful for their concern and help when I needed it. I was more than pleased to be able to return the favour.

Weng's three brothers and their families moved into small concrete houses with two rooms, plus a kitchen area each. I couldn't believe how cheap the rent was, at only £20 a month, so I paid the first month for them. They had to get their own furniture from friends.

It was time for me to head back to Singapore on my first leg home to the UK. All the family boarded the mini bus again to travel to Manila Airport. I looked out at the dusty roads and the passing ramshackle villages on the journey and felt a lump form in my throat. I didn't want to go home. I had found a new family and I was about to leave them, not knowing when I would see them again.

Weng and I had become very close friends over those 10 days, but it was only when I got back to Singapore that I realised that it was much more than that. I knew then that I had feelings for her and I hoped that she felt the same way about me.

I was due to stay over in Singapore for three days before returning to the UK, but when Weng and I spoke on the phone she told me that she missed me. I was overjoyed to hear that. Over the past few days I had had butterflies in my stomach and couldn't eat or sleep properly. I had never felt this way about a woman before and it scared me, but I was excited at the same time. Instead of getting on the plane to the UK, I booked a flight back to the Philippines.

26

Before I returned to the Philippines I went straight to Kenny in the studio in Singapore and asked him if I could record myself singing 'Unchained Melody' over the backing track for Weng as a surprise for her.

I bought an engagement ring from a smart jewellery shop and intended to propose properly this time around. I wanted the occasion to be romantic and memorable.

During the flight to Manila Airport I felt sick with nerves and could hardly swallow any of my cheese sandwich. I was like a love struck teenager.

When Weng and I spotted one another at the airport we fell into each other's arms.

"I missed you so much!" I said.

"I missed you, too!" Weng replied.

I knew right then that this was real, something that I had never experienced before. I loved Weng deeply.

That evening I asked her parents if I could have their daughter's hand in marriage. They agreed to my request after having a quick family meeting with Weng's brothers and Weng herself. I then produced the CD of 'Unchained Melody' and gave it to my intended. Out of my case I produced a small radio CD player which I had bought from the airport, as I noticed on my last visit that although Weng's family had CD's they had nothing to play them on. While the song crooned in the background I got down on one knee in Weng's parents living room. This time I was determined to do things in the right way. Weng deserved the best as far as I was concerned. I had just gone from the worse time in my life to the very happiest. And I had her to thank for that.

The ring was gold with a tiny diamond embedded in it and I held it up in its little purple box. I took a breath.

"Will you marry me?" I asked, looking up at Weng. Tears filled her eyes and I heard a sniffle to the side of me. When I looked at the rest of her family they were all crying and waiting for Weng to answer me. Suddenly she leaned down and hugged me.

"Of course I'll marry you!" she said.

"Oh good!" I laughed. "That's agreed then!"

With shaking hands I placed the engagement ring on her finger and we smiled at one another while the family clapped and chatted excitedly.

"I love you," I murmured.

"I love you too, Ron."

To celebrate, the next day I took the family to a place called Med's Resort, which had an outdoor swimming pool. There must have been about twenty of us including the kids and we tucked into a barbecue and got to know one another properly. They never got a chance to do things like that as they struggled to survive each day, but it was great to see all the smiling faces.

Weng had never been away from her family. Hers were very strict parents, she being the only daughter out of four children, but we plucked up courage to ask them if we could go to Singapore alone for a few days. So, once more, it was family meeting time to discuss our proposal.

Weng said that her parents would say no, however after a short discussion they announced that we could go together for our five day trip when we agreed that we would have separate rooms. I promised her mum and dad that my intentions were honourable. They knew I had a bad track record and seven wives behind me but I assured them that I had great respect for Weng and her family and I wasn't about to make the same mistakes again. So I made the arrangements with the hotel and booked the flights.

When Weng saw the Hotel Miramar in Singapore her face was a picture. It was a lavishly decorated place with mirrors and marble floors everywhere. Weng couldn't believe how big her room was. It was the first time she had been abroad.

"I feel like a princess being whisked away!" she said, giggling while she took in the thick brocade curtains at the large windows and the round bath.

We took a cable car to Sentosa, an adjoining Island which is part of Singapore, where we enjoyed all the attractions including a man-made beach and we walked across a rope foot bridge which you can cross to stand at the southern most point of South East Asia. The highlight of our visit was the Underwater World. We glided along on a moving escalator with sharks and stingrays almost in touching distance above us.

"I've never seen anything like it before, Ron!" Weng cried. "I can't believe it!"

I put my arm around her. "Are you enjoying yourself?"

"Oh yes!" she said. "I'm having the time of my life!"

I wanted to show Weng sights that she had only seen on TV. It was my way of saying thank you for all the kindness and for saving me.

Those five-days went very fast and it was time to head back to Manila where Weng's family were there to greet us at the airport. They wanted to know about the trip, so that night we sat down to watch our time in Singapore which I had recorded on a video camera.

Unfortunately I had to return to the UK because my visitor's visa would soon expire. But I didn't care. I knew that Weng loved me and we would be together. I even started wearing patches to help me quit smoking. Now that was something new for me, but I was determined to stop, mainly for my health but also for Weng and because none of her family smoked.

It was summer in Britain and the local radio station on the Isle of Wight invited me in for an interview about my upcoming nuptials, so I was live on the lunchtime phone-in, where members of the public were invited to call and air their views. Everyone wanted to know why I was looking for wife number eight and many people made harsh comments, particularly about the 30-year age gap.

After the breakdown of my marriage to Wan and the death of my mother I had been in no fit state to deal with the radio show and people's judgemental remarks but I felt stronger now. I could understand why people were interested to know about my unusual private life.

The local newspaper contacted me for an interview and also the local TV station. I was dubbed 'Britain's Most Married Man' again and one newspaper named me 'Lord of The Wedding Rings'. Weng was a celebrity before she even arrived in the UK. I got both of us an agent to deal with the media enquiries. Maggie Morgan worked for Solent News Agency in Southampton and was a real gem.

There was still a lot to do for me to get Weng over to the UK, as it was easier for us to marry here. We applied for a Fiancé Visa, which meant that we had to marry in the UK within six months of her arrival. The application was submitted in June 2004, but the embassy said she had to wait till November for her interview in Manila, as the waiting list was long. In the meantime Weng and I spent hours on the Internet chatting to each other, and on the phone. We were both frantic with worry and didn't want to wait that long to be together.

I decided to contact Home Secretary David Blunkett and Ian McCartney, who was a minister as well, so I wrote to them asking if they could help to speed up the process for Weng's application.

When I was campaigning for Arachnoiditis I had a lot of help from them both.

Six weeks passed and Weng and I spoke every day on the phone, often in tears because we missed one another so badly. After being granted a last minute appointment with the embassy because someone else cancelled we waited for some good news, but we were devastated when Weng was refused her Fiancée visa. We were baffled at first however it turned out that I had sent the wrong divorce certificate in with all the papers that I had to submit as her sponsor. The embassy stated that once I gave them the correct paper they would give her the visa under an appeals ruling.

Within a week I was back in the air to the Philippines, with the right document this time and feeling silly for my mistake. When I arrived it was all very tense, but everyone was glad to see me again, especially Weng, who ran into my arms at the airport.

A week later her visa was granted and a few days later it was time to say goodbye to her family, whom we promised we would visit the following year. Weng had mixed emotions; she wanted to be with me, but was sad to say goodbye to everyone.

As the plane made its way into the sky, I gripped Weng's hand and looked at her. "Are you OK?"

She nodded. "I love my family but I want to be with you."

"You excited?" I asked, smiling. My stomach was fluttering with nerves and had been for weeks.

"Oh yes!" she said. "I can't wait to get married."

We decided to stop over in Singapore for a couple of days and we visited Kenny in his studio. Shania Twain's, 'From This Moment' was special to us and we wanted to record it as a duet to play at our wedding. Weng had never been in a recording studio before, but Kenny mentioned how impressed he was with her voice and how professional she was.

On the 15th October 2004 we arrived in the UK and as soon as we set foot back on the Isle of Wight we began arranging our wedding. In the meantime, the media wanted stories and pictures of both of us and to know when we were getting married, and where. We were invited to the local radio station for an interview, hosted by Alex Dyke. Some of the listeners thought that Weng shouldn't marry me because of my track record. One even suggested that she would pay towards her airfare home and that other listeners do the same. Alex thought the show was a blast and couldn't see why we might be upset. It was the first time that I had seen Weng with anger in her eyes.

"This is so wrong!" she said to me after we left the studio. "Why are people being like this? We love one another!"

"I know. Take no notice," I soothed her. "Let's just concentrate on our big day."

"But it's so wrong!" she said.

"It doesn't matter what anyone else thinks. We know the truth," I reminded her.

Weng sighed. "But it's so frustrating…"

I gave her a hug and we went home.

The station wanted to know the date of our wedding, but we refused to tell them. We had already signed an agreement with 'The News of the World', which wanted the exclusive of our ceremony, so we had to keep the date and venue secret from everyone else. Unfortunately Isle of Wight radio station found out what date we were to marry and where it was happening. The press furore was quite a shock to both of us and my family, but we tried not to let it all affect our excitement, although my sister and her husband decided that it was too much for them and told us that they would be keeping away from the wedding. I didn't blame them. The Isle of Wight was a small place and it irritated me that strangers were following us and shouting out comments everywhere we went. But it wasn't all negative. Premier Ford offered us the use of two cars for the day, free of charge, and Pontins gave us a four-day honeymoon at one of their centres.

However, the local radio station then announced that they were going to be there with a live outside broadcast, fronted by Alex Dyke. When I heard that I called the registrar and told them that we didn't want the station broadcasting the service; that we only wanted the photographer of the News of the World to take photographs in the registry office, who were also doing our own wedding shots. The registrar organised some security to be present at the ceremony.

Finally, the big day arrived – the 15th November 2004. A guy called Steve was sent from the newspaper to look after us and keep other journalists at bay.

Photographers and TV crews surrounded Weng as she got out of the wedding car. They thrust microphone booms in her face and barked questions, but she was rushed in quickly by the security without answering anything. To avoid any press intrusion, Weng and I entered the Newport Register Office by the back door at different times, and when I first spotted her across the room in her finery I was overcome with emotion. She wore a cream silk wedding dress and was carrying orchids and wearing one in her hair. I thought she looked beautiful. I was all done up in a black tuxedo with bow tie with a red rose in my lapel.

Some of our guests were asked to take photographs of us by different national and local newspapers, having been promised that they would pay them for the photo. So Steve and the registrar banned all cameras and mobile phones, except the guy from the News of The World. Isle of Wight Radio was banned from broadcasting and from entering the register office.

Finally, to the sound of us singing 'From This Moment' on our pre-recorded disk, Weng and I took our places at the front of the room, which was decorated with vases of colourful flowers. The music gently faded as the lady registrar welcomed a handful of our closest friends we had invited, and the ceremony began.

I could feel tears welling up in my eyes when I looked at Weng, but I managed to control myself by taking a few deep breaths. The words "I now pronounce you man and wife" really stood out for me during the service. The past was behind me. I had found the love of my life.

Epilogue

Weng and I had a wonderful honeymoon at Pontins Holiday Centre in Pakefield, Suffolk. We smooched to slow tunes in the ballroom in the evenings and I introduced Weng to bingo. It was nice not to be calling out the numbers this time. But I was puzzled as to why Weng kept leaning over and telling me what numbers I had on my card.

"Why aren't you watching your own card?" I asked her.

"Mine's all full up," she said.

I laughed out loud. "That means you've got a full house!"

"What does that mean?" Weng was frowning.

"You've won!" I said.

"I've won?"

"Yes!" I cried and stood, waving the card in the air towards the bingo caller. "Full house, mate! Oi, over 'ere!"

"Why are you shouting like that?" Weng asked, looking more confused than ever.

I explained the rules of the game and told her to expect a prize any minute. She looked excited at this prospect; although I knew holiday camps well enough to realize that she wouldn't be going home with a brand new car or set of posh luggage. But when Weng was presented with a jar of rose scented bath salts I was shocked to see that the glow of her windfall was still showing on her face long afterwards.

"I've never won anything before," she smiled, hugging her prize to her chest. I had never loved her more.

After the honeymoon and Christmas with Weng's family in the Philippines in 2004 we settled in well to married life, but the constant press intrusion on the island was exhausting. Isle of Wight radio continued to run phone-in shows about us and everyone kept asking if we were still together or if we had divorced yet. It was as if they were waiting for us to fail. We were constantly hassled by people on the street, in shops and even at traffic lights. Alex Dyke, the radio presenter, never tired of raking over the details of my love life, which was especially galling considering he had tried to ruin our day by barging into our wedding before and after the ceremony. I wondered when he would tire of fueling gossip about me. He was scraping the bottom of the barrel for stories, I thought. I wasn't exactly Rod Stewart. I couldn't get my head around it. Yes, I had invited press attention over the years but it was getting silly.

Now I was with Weng I wanted us to have some peace in which to begin our lives together. We decided to move to Somerton, Somerset, which is a picturesque village. We fell in love with it at once and no one there knew about my past so we were able to make friends and blend in like any other couple. We live there to this day.

Weng got a job in a care home for the elderly in Street, Somerset, and she became the Deputy Manager. We have been happily married for almost 10 years and spend our evenings going to rehearsals for fellowship in our Church, where we both sing together in the worship band. We enjoy watching films, singing karaoke and going for drives and doing a spot of fishing in the summer. I am 65 and Weng is 35. The age gap has never been an issue for us. Our connection goes deeper than age or anything like that. We both believe that Weng was sent to save me and that we are meant to be together. Call it fate if you like. Our shared faith keeps us strong.

We visit Weng's family when we can and they came over for Christmas 2011. It was wonderful to see them all.

Weng and I are still in demand with the media. I thought they would have forgotten about us as soon as they realised we wouldn't be heading to the divorce courts, but we are often offered chat shows and documentaries, including a programme called *New Brittania* for Sky Atlantic, which is about relationships.

I *am* Britain's Most Married Man after all, so I have to expect people to clamour to get my sound advice on such sensitive subjects. Who else can say they have spent so much time in a register office? But I won't be caught with a ninth wife. No way. I have found the woman I was meant to be with and I have had my fill of wedding cake.

In 2005 my two sons from my third marriage, Lee and Craig, saw an article featuring Shane Richie and me in a newspaper and thankfully got in touch, which meant that I had been reunited with seven of my eight children, who range in age from 23 to 44. I have 12 grandchildren and one great grandchild and am a very proud granddad. I love all my family dearly.

Lorraine, my youngest daughter from the marriage with my first wife Margaret refused to have anything to do with me and has said she will contact me once Weng and I have been married for 10 years. I saw her at my mother's funeral in 2004 and that was it. I can't say I ever blamed her, but I always wanted her to know that I'm a changed man and she means so much to me.

Luckily I didn't have to wait the full decade to be reunited with Lorraine. I was a year from the deadline when something surprising happened. A few months ago Weng and I were invited to my niece's wedding blessing and I found out that Lorraine and her daughter were going to be there. I had never seen six-year-old Hermione and my stomach was in knots, wondering how my daughter would react to me. On the day, as Weng and I got done up in our best togs, I prayed that I would be granted my wish and get the rest of my family back.

Along with other family members, we had to go to Lorraine's caravan prior to the ceremony, which happened to be near to where ours was situated at Cheverton Holiday Park on the Isle of Wight. When we first saw one another I could see the tension on Lorraine's face and I must have looked petrified as well, I was so uptight, but then Lorraine and I started asking each other how we were keeping, especially as I knew she had been unwell of late.

Then out of another room came Hermione. Blonde haired and with the same neat facial features, she looked exactly like her mother at that age and a lump formed in my throat. It was like I had gone back in time. She ran up to me and gave me a smile and a huge hug. How wonderful it was to have this little girl I had never met treat me like she had known me since she was born. I felt tears well in the corner of my eyes. Hermione smiled again and kissed me on the cheek; she even followed me when someone else spoke to me and I said I would see her later. Still choked, I looked at my little granddaughter and wondered if she had felt some sort of instinctive closeness or natural bond towards me, knowing I was her granddad. I don't know but I was overwhelmed by her actions and I hoped that Lorraine, Hermione and I could make up for lost time and be a proper family. However, little did I realise that I had an important lesson to be taught first – and one that I should have learnt long before.

After the blessing there was an evening do at a local hall and Lorraine and I were chatting in a friendly manner when my son Dennis, from my ex-wife Sharon, came over to join us. After a brief chat, Lorraine leaned forward with an elbow on the table, looked seriously at me and said, "now listen to me, Ron, erm, Dad, erm Ron, sorry, Dad. In the past it has all been about you, you, you." She glanced at Dennis and he nodded and gave me a nod, his eyes darting in his sister's direction. Lorraine carried on, "now it's time for you to listen to us, that's if you want this relationship with me to continue."

It was always about me they both reiterated: "Not what we want or what we want to say to you. It was all *I, I, I*."

When they had finished saying their piece it dawned on me that what they were saying was absolutely true. Why hadn't I seen it before? For the first time in my life I realised how selfish and ignorant I had been, and that was hard to take; it was like a punch in the belly. I was ashamed. Agreeing with them both, I apologized and promised things would be different, and I thought about what they had said long after that evening. I could have kicked myself for my past mistakes. I'd made so many. How I hoped that I would get a chance to make it up to my family.

Well, I did get that opportunity and I consider myself a lucky man. Now Lorraine and I see one another, speak on the phone, chat online and do all the usual things in a daughter and father relationship. I have been in touch with Dennis for years and still see him too. They have grown into such lovely people and I couldn't be prouder of them. I feel sad though; that I had missed out on seeing my kids grow up and being around when my grandaugter was born. How I wish I could go back in time and do everything properly.

I know I have not been the perfect dad or granddad and I should have been stronger and given them the attention and other things that kids need, but I am pleased to say that all my children stay in touch with each other. Although they are half brothers and sisters they see each other when they can. I would like to say sorry to them for all those times that I wasn't there or if I hurt them.

Weng had first noticed my hands would sometimes shake when we met back in 2004 but she didn't mention it then. I had also spotted it, but as I wasn't dropping or spilling things I took little notice of it – and it wasn't like I was a big drinker, so I couldn't put it down to my love of the pub. I never went in those places.

As the years went on, if I was carrying a cup of tea I found I was spilling a little and I began to worry more about it. So when I saw the doctor he said it was nerves and gave me anti depressants but still the shakes carried on and I simply put up with it until it got to a point where it was interfering in my life. I went back to my GP and said that I had noticed that my legs were shaking sometimes when I was sitting down and that the tremors were making it difficult to rest and sleep. He referred me to a neuro-consultant.

After a few elementary tests it was concluded that I had Essential Tremor Syndrome, so, seeing it as nothing too serious, he asked to see me six months later. By then I had muscular pains in my joints too, but he wasn't too concerned and said he would see me again in three months.

With the episodes of pain and weakness in my muscles, along with the slowness in my walking and added shuffling, the doctor began to take me more seriously. I was sent for a DAT scan at Frenchay Hospital Bristol on 23rd May 2013 which just happened to be my 65th birthday. What a way to celebrate, I thought while having a radiation injection stuck into my arm and lying there under the scanner.

I was sent a letter with an appointment date, to get the results on 20th July 2013, which was quite an alarmingly long time to wait for such news. As the day approached I was a bag of nerves, as was Weng.

We sat down in the consultant's office and looked at him. His face was sympathetic while he peered at us; he took a deep breath and said, "I'm afraid the results have come back positive. You have Parkinson's Disease."

Although Weng and I had suspected it was PD, as had the medics, because my mother had suffered from it late in life, and I was stumbling and had stiffening of the limbs, there was something inside me that kept hoping that I couldn't possibly be diagnosed with a condition like that. Not me. But there it was. It was true.

As the consultant said he was sorry and gave us more sympathetic looks, Weng and I held hands while we cried. I couldn't get my head around it, immediately fearing for my future independence, knowing it was a progressive disease. That was the worst part. I was already having problems with things like drying my feet after a shower and putting my socks on and driving was becoming more of a challenge. Luckily Weng was there to take over such tasks for me.

The consultant tried to reassure us both, reminding us that with new medications it could slow up the progression but I would have to be patient as the meds he was going to put me on would have to be increased very slowly until I could receive the full benefit of them, which will possibly take a year.

So, along with medication, I have rehab therapy, and have received so much support with this condition since it was diagnosed. The staff at Frenchay Hospital has been amazing. Occupational therapists have provided a wheelchair for when I need to use it and I have a specialist Parkinson's nurse.

My attitude is that I have to accept it and stay positive and that is what I am concentrating on right now. The shakes make it hard for me to sleep but I have to hope that the right level of medication will be found for me and that eventually a cure will be discovered. I am not giving up. I refuse to let this beat me down. Our faith keeps my wife and me going.

In 2011 Weng decided that she wanted to go into adult nursing, so she gave her job up as Deputy Manager in a residential care home and applied to do an Access to Higher Education one year college course in Somerset. While there she applied to Bournemouth University to take a nursing degree. Weng worked really hard on the consignments she had to pass to get into Bournemouth and eighteen months later she was accepted by the university having attained top marks from her college in Somerset, getting 15 out of 16 distinctions, and the other a merit. She has just started at Bournemouth University and has three years of study and training. I'm so proud of her and I know she will make a wonderful nurse. It is something she has always wanted to do.

As for Frank Bush, I sometimes still think of him but my past doesn't haunt me like it used to and I'm relieved that I have finally told the truth about what happened when I was a child. A great burden has been lifted off of me. Weng has been at my side throughout all of this and I can't begin to thank her enough for her ongoing support.

I sincerely hope that my admission encourages others to tell someone if they are suffering sexual abuse. I wish I had spoken out much sooner. When I see pedophile cases on the news it makes me angry that the perpetrators often receive such pathetic prison sentences. These monsters ruin people's lives. If I could turn back the clock I would like to see Frank Bush in jail. It worries me greatly that he targeted others.

It is also my hope that by reading this book someone will find the courage to realise that they aren't alone and that no one needs to keep anything so terrible bottled up for so long. If I could speak to that nine-year-old boy I used to be I'd tell him to go to his parents, a teacher, the police, anyone. Please don't put up with it.

As for life now, I have good days and bad days with my condition, but there is always somebody worse off than you I tell myself and God is watching over me and taking care of me and my family. I have been blessed with a beautiful and caring wife and I am thankful every day for what we have found in one another. We are happy and content.

Green coats and bingo balls lost their appeal for me years ago. However, I still do the odd Frank Spencer or Norman Wisdom impression if pushed, or I feel the urge. These days I am retired but I spend my time helping new young talent to follow their dreams. I utilize my 50 years in show business well and introduce them to my contacts; after all it's not what you know but who you know. If I can give a little back to the business then I'm happy to help talented unknowns break through so they can achieve their career ambitions.

Things are vastly different for me now and I enjoy a quiet life with Weng. My days of philandering are a dim and distant memory. I can honestly say that I love being a married man and cannot recommend it highly enough, though if I had to offer some marriage advice: eight times might be a few too many. All my wives were lovely people but I have found who I was meant to be with. And I'm extremely proud to say that I'm a retired Romeo.